Patient
No Longer

Patient
No Longer

*Why Healthcare Must Deliver
the Care Experience That
Consumers Want and Expect*

Ryan Donohue | Stephen K. Klasko

ACHE Management Series

Your board, staff, or clients may also benefit from this book's insight. For information on quantity discounts, contact the Health Administration Press Marketing Manager at (312) 424-9450.

Library of Congress Cataloging-in-Publication Data
Names: Donohue, Ryan, author. | Klasko, Stephen K., author.
Title: Patient no longer : why healthcare must deliver the care experience that consumers want and expect / Ryan Donohue, Stephen K. Klasko.
Other titles: Management series (Ann Arbor, Mich.)
Description: Chicago, IL : Health Administration Press, [2021] | Series: HAP/ACHE management series | Includes bibliographical references and index. | Summary: "This book discusses the compelling reasons consumer-centric healthcare is so crucial and how healthcare leaders can work to build health systems focused on it"—Provided by publisher.
Identifiers: LCCN 2020013961 (print) | LCCN 2020013962 (ebook) | ISBN 9781640551800 (paperback ; alk. paper) | ISBN 9781640551824 (epub) | ISBN 9781640551831 (mobi) | ISBN 9781640551848 (xml)
Subjects: MESH: Patient-Centered Care—organization & administration | Consumer Behavior | Quality Improvement—organization & administration | United States
Classification: LCC RA418 (print) | LCC RA418 (ebook) | NLM W 84.7 | DDC 362.1—dc23
LC record available at https://lccn.loc.gov/2020013961
LC ebook record available at https://lccn.loc.gov/2020013962

The paper used in this publication meets the minimum requirements of American National Standard for Information Sciences—Permanence of Paper for Printed Library Materials, ANSI Z39.48-1984. ♾ ™

Acquisitions editor: Jennette McClain; Manuscript editor: Janice Snider; Project manager: Andrew Baumann; Cover designer: James Slate; Layout: Integra

Found an error or a typo? We want to know! Please e-mail it to hapbooks@ache.org, mentioning the book's title and putting "Book Error" in the subject line.

For photocopying and copyright information, please contact Copyright Clearance Center at www.copyright.com or at (978) 750-8400.

Health Administration Press
A division of the Foundation of the American
    College of Healthcare Executives
300 S. Riverside Plaza, Suite 1900
Chicago, IL 60606-6698
(312) 424-2800

Contents

Preface

HEALTHCARE MAY BE the first industry that will be forever transformed by coronavirus disease 2019 (COVID-19), but it won't be the last.

Every industry must now transform itself to create an equitable, sustainable business model that will allow it to thrive in an increasingly digital age after COVID-19. Quite simply, the Fourth Industrial Revolution—when online meets offline—has been intensified by this pandemic.

Just look at what happened to telehealth. Once a luxury, in March 2020 telehealth suddenly became the primary mode of seeking care.

At my institution, the Jefferson telehealth team began calling themselves the "Night's Watch," a reference to the *Game of Thrones* border army. And they were right—telehealth tackled the first wave of the virus that causes COVID-19.

The result has changed medicine forever. In January, before the coronavirus crisis, Jefferson's telehealth program helped 40–50 people per day who used its app to call an emergency medicine physician. By the last week of March, calls exceeded 1,200 per day—all of them from people who were sick and worried about COVID-19. Getting help by video screen saved them a trip to a doctor that could be difficult—and for many who are sick and older, very risky. Many such trips will never again be made in person.

Just as in healthcare, this pandemic will affect all businesses for at least 18 months, and most likely forever. It will require every sector to work closely with employees to reengineer the delivery of goods and services in an age when the traditional organization of workplaces will change, and when the nature of work itself will change.

From our perspective in healthcare delivery, here are my key learnings:

- **Digital tools for delivery of services must be robust and clearly communicated to customers and staff alike.** For example, pregnant women are already afraid to visit hospitals for prenatal care. Whereas home pregnancy monitors used to be a luxury, they will now rapidly become part of a new mode of pregnancy: digital diagnostic tools combined with the wisdom of obstetricians and pediatricians, many times offered virtually.

- **A vast reskilling of service jobs will be needed in the world of artificial intelligence.** In healthcare, we're now seeing thousands of physicians learning how to deliver sophisticated medicine through virtual visits. That kind of learning will occur in every industry.

- **We must put people first.** Ethics must not be an afterthought but rather considered at the beginning of new product development, before a new digital product goes to market. COVID-19 arrived during a crisis of trust; surveys by Edelman (2020) and others have found a deep mistrust of social institutions and traditional elites. Some of this mistrust is caused by the digital revolution itself—the fear that collected information may be used against oneself. We must earn trust at every stage.

- **We must reinvent how we protect the people who work for us.** COVID-19 has shattered the gig economy and the jobs of hourly employees in the service industry, and it has even injured those with full-time employment. In every crisis of the twentieth century, business and government leaders worked to "cover" employees by providing insurance for sickness, creating rules for employment status, and the like. The COVID-19 crisis demands similar leadership. The recovery of the economy in 2020 and beyond demands a new compact with those who do the work. This will be the single biggest concern of voters in the US elections of November 2020, and it will resonate throughout the world as the global economy rebuilds.

There is nothing positive or optimistic about large, enveloped RNA viruses such as the coronavirus. This time is a trying one for our nation and the world. But although the war against the virus may be won with drugs and vaccines, the fight for an equitable and sustainable global economy has just begun.

In healthcare, telehealth worked. Providing guidance to families worked. Listening worked. Even under our greatest threat since World War II, the principles of using digital medicine turned out to be critical. The coronavirus pandemic has validated the principles of this book: that we need healthcare with no address, helping people where they are and when they need it.

—*Stephen K. Klasko, MD, MBA*
President, Thomas Jefferson University
CEO, Jefferson Health

REFERENCE

Edelman. 2020. "2020 Edelman Trust Barometer." Published January 19. www.edelman.com/trustbarometer.

Acknowledgments

I WOULD LIKE to acknowledge my wife, Andrea, a wonderful woman who is always there for me and admirably stepped up to care for our children while I was consumed by the writing process. And to my three children, Ryan Jr., Winnie, and Maggie, for being three little sparks of joy and, perhaps most important, not being too hard on Mom while Dad was writing. I love you all.

—*Ryan Donohue*

This book is a labor of love, and I would like to give a shout-out to several people:

To my three marvelous children, Lynne, David, and Jill, who expect and hope that those of us responsible for the healthcare ecosystem will finally get it right in helping all people stay healthy.

To my wife, Colleen, who allows me to keep the light on late at night when I work on books and papers.

And my greatest thanks to the team who envisioned and assembled this book: Jona Raasch and Kathryn Peisert at The Governance Institute along with Ryan Donohue, and my colleague Michael Hoad at Jefferson Health.

In essence, this book is dedicated to all of you who seek what we all want for ourselves and our families—health assurance—the ability to thrive without having health get in the way.

—*Stephen K. Klasko, MD, MBA*

The original idea and encouragement to write this book came from three individuals who have spent their entire careers building cultures that are, first and foremost, patient centered: Richard Buck, MD, Michael Bleich, PhD, RN, FAAN, and Tamera Mahaffey, NP. We appreciate their early meetings with us, discussing how to build on the book *Through the Patient's Eyes*, a gift to our industry, by providing us with a way to understand and promote patient-centered care through the patient's eyes. We benefited greatly from their advice to do more than just update the book's content and show what, if any, progress the industry has made in improving the patient experience. To truly do what is best for patients, we need to change ourselves first and then move from a patient-centered industry to a consumer-obsessed industry. To do this, you have to have human understanding. We knew the research would show that the original Picker dimensions of care are still as relevant and as important to patients today as they were 25 years ago. And we have taken the liberty to show how they are important to consumers.

None of this work would have been possible without Harvey and Jean Picker's insight into the need for research to create the original Picker dimensions and ensure that they were used to help drive improvement and not just measurement. Harvey was supportive and engaged in making sure the Picker work continued in the hands of NRC Health and internationally. We will be forever grateful for his ongoing encouragement and participation until his death in 2008. Gail Warden was also instrumental in continuing the Picker work with his role on the Picker Institute board and on the NRC Health board. We benefited greatly from his support, guidance, and insights into how great leaders lead and how you create a patient-centered culture that constantly develops leaders and providers who put the patient first while supporting and growing a community that understands the importance of how social determinants affect health.

We also would like to thank Dr. Stephen Klasko and Michael Hoad at Jefferson Health. We knew the minute we met Dr. Klasko that he was a forward-thinking and an innovative leader. We have benefited from our many interactions and enjoyed observing what a truly driven, positive, futuristic, and committed leader can do regardless of his or her address. Michael Hoad gifted us with his writing and brilliant advice.

We also thank all the associates at NRC Health, who are passionate about our mission and dedicated to helping our clients deliver not only patient-centered care but also human understanding. Finally, we are grateful to Mike Hays, our founder and CEO, who has insisted that we remain "outside-in," focused on what is right, and that we always make others successful and look for solutions.

—*Ryan Donohue, Jona Raasch, Megan Charko, Jennifer Volland, Katherine Johnson, and Kathryn C. Peisert NRC Health, Lincoln, Nebraska*

Introduction

Stephen K. Klasko, MD, MBA

IN THE 1980s, 1990s, and 2000s, patient centeredness resided in the marketing department of hospitals. "We are patient centered," the billboards exclaimed. But we were all missing the point. "We" includes providers, insurers, hospitals, pharmaceutical companies, and even patients. The real question is why healthcare has escaped the consumer revolution these past 30 years and why we are so self-congratulatory when we make baby steps in that direction.

This book explores the why, and more importantly what we can do about it, in a meaningful and data-driven way. It assumes that the "service" we give patients today will be laughable ten years from now and explores how we can start the revolution toward consumer-centric care. The title and body of this book focus on *consumer* centricity, not patient centeredness, because, in our experience, words matter. Patients are sick and need care for their diseases. Consumers expect the kind of service they receive in other industries, regardless of whether they are ill or healthy.

The premise upon which this book is built is that we are going through a once-in-an-era change in healthcare, from a business-to-business model to a business-to-consumer model. In other words, healthcare is in the midst of a shift from a wholesale model, where providers sell themselves to physicians and insurers, to a retail model, where providers sell themselves directly to consumers. Today, employers still make most benefit decisions on behalf of individuals and their families. Tomorrow, individuals will make decisions about benefits, providers, and their course of care. To put it simply, things change when you are not using OPM (other people's money). The combination of more sophisticated consumers, the popularity of government-managed insurance and even "Medicare for All," the need to be bold and think differently or go bankrupt, and the rise of high-deductible plans on the commercial side will move the system from a "house money" mentality to one in which consumers make decisions the same way they do in other aspects of their lives—namely, with an "it's my money" mentality.

Once we make the leap from physician and administrator as the boss to patient as the boss, everything changes. The healthcare ecosystem moves from hospital companies or insurance companies to consumer healthcare entities. The writers of this book recognize that now is the time to actualize the pioneering work done by Harvey Picker and the Picker Institute, as described in *Through the Patient's Eyes*. That work changed my perspective as a physician and led to my desire to run a large healthcare system through the consumers' eyes.

Any business CEO will tell you that failing to be consumer centric is the biggest threat to survival. Transformative businesses such as Amazon, Netflix, Uber, Apple, and Airbnb would not exist if the retail industry, Blockbuster, the taxi industry, the music industry, or the hotel industry had realized that bad customer service, ridiculous fees, and limited availability and pricing options have a short shelf life in our age of acceleration. In *Unscaled*, Hemant Taneja (2018) discusses how technology coupled with economics is unraveling behemoth industries—including corporations, banks, farms, media conglomerates, energy systems, governments, and schools—that have long dominated business and society. Size and scale have become a liability.

What happens when you begin to look through the consumer's eyes? For a start, ask them. A recent unpublished survey of patients at Jefferson Health asked if healthcare was like other aspects of life, and their passion and near consensus were somewhat surprising:

- 71 percent expect physicians to have online scheduling with comparative rates.
- 65 percent expect that there will be social networking opportunities to discuss health-related topics and compare providers.
- 92 percent expect to have full two-way electronic communication with their providers.
- 83 percent expect that they will be able to access all their patient information as they do their bank accounts online.
- 78 percent expect to have total access to family members' inpatient charts and that they will be able to participate in rounds in-person or virtually.

Through the consumer's eyes, healthcare is not that complicated. People want a seamless, personalized experience where technology such as genomics and augmented intelligence is used in a way that gives them more control over their disease or their health; where physicians are not "captains of the ship" but partners in health; and where they are understood and treated as human beings with emotional needs in addition to their physical needs. Hospitals should not be imposing places where hospitality is forgotten, and insurers should not be barriers between the patient and provider. As you read this book, you will realize that the market forces of consumer centricity, new definitions of patient satisfaction, reduction of OPM, rise of the millennial factor (namely, technology over blind loyalty), and an increasing buyer's market with more options will lead to a future where those of us in the healthcare ecosystem must meet the needs of patients to consume healthcare in the same flexible manner in which they consume every other consumer good.

As the leader of a large healthcare system, I will live or die based on our care and caring, not our location or bricks and mortar. Former Apple CEO John Sculley admonished us to stop using terms like *telehealth*, stating that we don't talk about *telebanking* (oral communication, July 2017). Banking and finance have morphed from an industry where everything was done at the bank to one where more than 80 percent of banking is done at home or remotely with a variety of technologies.

Viewing the healthcare revolution from the consumer's eyes involves taking a leap into what will be obvious ten years from now and doing it today. Not only is this the right thing to do for your patients, but it's also great business. Guide consumers by giving them the information they need to make good decisions about their health. Simply put, consumers who are disengaged in their own healthcare are often unsatisfied and drive up costs. Find convenient ways for consumers to connect with your healthcare ecosystem. Amazon, Target, and Walmart recognize that they need to connect with consumers even when they are not in the store. Most of all, inspire loyalty by learning from the success of other consumer-facing industries; demonstrate value, especially with respect to a patient's own money; give consumers a single point of contact; and create a seamless experience across the continuum.

As you read this book, view it as a guidepost for an optimistic future—a future in which healthcare does not have an address, but one where consumers and providers partner together to create healthier communities. That goal is attainable. *You* have the power to change the current dynamics. This book can serve as the beginning of the journey.

REFERENCE

Taneja, H., with K. Maney. 2018. *Unscaled: How AI and a New Generation of Upstarts Are Creating the Economy of the Future.* New York: Public Affairs.

PART I

History and Healthcare Context of Patient-Centered Care

CHAPTER 1

How We Got Here: A Brief History of Patient-Centered Care

IT WAS THE worst of surgeries, it was the best of surgeries. . . . Tim and Suzi had been married for 40 years and enjoyed good health and active lifestyles. Tim played golf, was caregiver to his four grandchildren, and did regular work tending to his sizeable garden. Retired, he kept busy helping other family members and members of his church community in various ways.

Neither Tim nor Suzi had much reason to encounter the healthcare industry in their more than 40 years of marriage. Their two children had been born with no complications and normal deliveries. Both Tim and Suzi saw a primary care physician and received medical screening tests and physicals recommended for their age.

But when Tim went in for his annual physical at age 62, his blood test showed an elevated prostate-specific antigen (PSA) score. It was slightly higher six months later, so his physician recommended he see a urologist. At the urologist appointment just a few weeks later, another blood test revealed that Tim's score on the Gleason scale was on the border of being considered cancerous. A biopsy showed cancer cells in 4 of the 12 samples, and the urologist encouraged Tim to have his prostate removed. The urologist pressed hard, saying that because Tim was active and in excellent health, he should make a complete recovery. Tim was reluctant, as his father had had his prostate removed 20 years prior, never regained normal control, and regretted having had the surgery.

Suzi questioned the urologist because she knew that the United States had more stringent recommendations for PSA testing and prostate surgery than other countries did, even though the number of deaths due to prostate cancer was no higher in other countries. Both Tim and Suzi expressed their concerns about Tim's father's experience. The urologist emphasized the many medical advances made in the past 20 years and explained that, with robotic surgery, he was confident there would be no problems. Tim and Suzi considered getting another opinion, but after Tim thought further about it, he decided he wanted to get it over with; he wanted to recover fully by January so that he would not have to miss marshalling at the PGA tournament in San Diego, a favorite activity of his that had become a cherished tradition.

Tim needed an electrocardiogram (EKG) and an additional blood test to get a sign-off from his primary care physician prior to surgery. He had to make these appointments on his own, all while thinking about the major surgery ahead of him. He didn't understand why another blood test was needed, as he had just had one prior to his urologist visit. During the EKG, Tim was asked when he had had a heart attack, even though he had never had one. After much discussion and further examination by his physician, he was sent to a local cardiology clinic to have yet another EKG to ensure everything was OK prior to surgery. Finally, after further difficult testing that didn't make any sense to Tim and enduring additional appointments, scheduling challenges, and great expense, he was assured nothing was wrong with his heart and was cleared for surgery.

When the time came, Tim's surgeon explained to Tim and Suzi what to expect in the hospital and emphasized again that, because it was robotic surgery, Tim could expect a speedy and complete recovery. He was told the biggest inconvenience he would experience was having a catheter for seven to ten days after surgery.

Tim came through surgery with no problems. He was up and walking right away and quickly got accustomed to the catheter. He looked forward to going home. Hospital staff members were polite, but when Tim asked questions, they often replied, "Who is your surgeon? Oh, you have Dr. Jones. Well, he likes things done a certain way." This response made Tim wonder if his surgeon was different from most and how other surgeons did things, and it caused him some fear and anxiety. Also, depending on which nurse he asked, he received different answers to the same questions. There was no sense of teamwork or coordination.

Tim's first week home went according to plan, and he looked forward to his first follow-up visit to have the catheter removed. Everything checked out fine, and the physician seemed pleased with Tim's progress. But since Tim had expected to return to normal fairly quickly, and his physician had told him he was healing nicely, he became frustrated when he didn't regain his normal urinary control. Tim expressed this concern at his three-week follow-up visit and was told, for the first time, that it could take 9 to 12 months to get back to normal. This news came as a shock to both Tim and Suzi—this didn't sound like a "speedy and complete recovery" to them. It made them wonder what else they had not been told.

Around this time, Suzi began waking up frequently at night with what seemed to be stomach cramps. She thought she might be having a reaction to the acidic nature of all the fresh garden vegetables she and Tim had been enjoying recently. She also felt it might be stress caused by Tim's delayed recovery. But after about a month, the discomfort became longer and more intense and felt more like menstrual cramps, so Suzi scheduled an appointment with her obstetrician/gynecologist (ob-gyn). During the week she had to wait for the appointment, her pain became even more severe, lasting several hours at a time. Her ob-gyn scheduled an ultrasound for her. While driving back to work after the ultrasound, Suzi received a phone call from the technician, who said that the physician wanted to see her the next day in her office. At the visit, Suzi learned that her uterus was extremely enlarged—to 18 inches, compared to the normal uterus size of 3 to 4 inches. The increase in size concerned Suzi because, two years prior, she had had a dilation and curettage procedure to remove fibroids that were causing heavy bleeding and discomfort, and at the time the physician said her uterus was 14 inches. The consensus was that Suzi's uterus needed to be removed. Although Suzi's ob-gyn conducted a lot of hysterectomies, she wanted to consult with a specialist in a nearby city who conducted robotic hysterectomies; she wanted to see if he could do the surgery, as it would be a safer option in the event that cancer was involved.

Suzi was prescribed painkillers to help with the painful nights. A few days later, she and Tim met with the specialist and learned that the robotic procedure was in fact possible. The surgery was scheduled for the following week, and all necessary presurgical tests were handled and coordinated that day in the specialist's office. Tim and Suzi left with everything handled and scheduled for them. The only remaining challenge was managing the increasing pain until the surgery. On Sunday, the day before Suzi was to check into the hospital, her pain was so severe that she called the surgeon's office and spoke with the on-call physician. He recommended that she drive to the hospital and be admitted through the emergency department. There, Suzi was quickly set up with an intravenous morphine drip, which relieved her pain immediately. Soon thereafter, she was admitted the room she would occupy for the balance of her hospital stay. Once in her room, two nurses introduced themselves and explained that they were part of her surgeon's team. They confirmed that her surgery was scheduled for the next morning and explained that they were there to help manage the pain and prepare her for surgery the next day. That night, Suzi had her first hours of pain-free sleep in several weeks.

She came through surgery extremely well despite complications caused by the size of the uterus, and her surgeon had no concerns. Once back in her room, Suzi was up and walking and felt the best she had in over a month. Tim and her children had left by then, as it had been a very early morning and a long day. Suzi's nurses said she was doing so well that she would be ready to return home that evening or the next morning. Suzi decided to wait for Tim's planned return in the morning and not make him drive an hour back late at night. Everything was completely ready for her discharge the next morning. Suzi received full explanations of what to expect and when, and she was given options whenever possible.

Suzie's experience was extremely well coordinated, and all her health providers were members of the same team—Suzi's team. There was never any delay or waiting for answers. Everyone seemed focused on helping Suzi manage her pain and return home for a restful recovery. The team handled all appointments, always taking her preferences into consideration and making her feel like she was everyone's top priority. In contrast, Tim's experience was not at all coordinated. The burden was put on him to schedule, coordinate, call, explain and re-explain, and insist that his appointments be made in time for surgery. It was his responsibility to think of and ask every question possible, as the only information shared concerned the clinical process of the surgery. Tim was given neither time nor the opportunity to explore treatment options; in fact, he was given no treatment options other than surgery.

* * *

As an industry, healthcare can be mysterious. On the outside, it gives off a cold feel. It's a world you won't have to visit much, if you're lucky and healthy. That perception is not lost on its leaders. For decades, healthcare CEOs, experts, and consultants have banged the collective drum to become more compassionate, more convenient, and more in line with the belief that care should be centered around the patient.

The latest charge for "patient-centered care" came in 2005, during a time when healthcare was coming to grips with rising costs and stagnating quality of care. The term *value-based care* was still not widely used or understood. The patient-centered charge made it all the way to Washington, DC, and politicians listened.

In December 2005, the Office of Management and Budget gave its final approval for the national implementation of the Hospital Consumer Assessment of Healthcare Providers and Systems (HCAHPS) surveys for public reporting purposes. When the Centers for Medicare & Medicaid Services (CMS) began tying a portion of hospital Medicare payments to survey scores in 2007, hospitals started to pay more attention. A widespread effort was put in place to give patients a voice and to improve healthcare for patients. The first public reporting of HCAHPS results occurred in March 2008 (CMS 2020).

After more than a decade of efforts to improve the patient experience, what do we have to show for it? Has widespread measurement of the patient experience created actionable data and real-life improvement? Has the call to consider the patient's point of view shifted minds—and hearts—to what's most important in healthcare? Has an entirely new industry of patient-focused educational and training tactics staffed hospitals with newer, kinder caregivers? To answer these critical questions, we must first revisit the most prolific study of patient-centered care in US history.

THE WORK OF HARVEY PICKER

Born into a healthcare family, Harvey Picker didn't set out to change the industry—at least not initially. Picker followed in his father's footsteps and took the reins of Picker X-Ray, a leading-edge X-ray technology company that aided Allied efforts in World War II and saved lives with small, nearly indestructible imaging machines that could be used almost anywhere. Picker devoted three decades of his adult life to the business that bore his father's name. His wife, Jean, was a US ambassador to the United Nations, an acclaimed journalist for *Life* magazine, and a personal friend of Eleanor Roosevelt.

Picker spoke to a London *Times* reporter in 2006. According to the published article, "the couple's personal experiences of healthcare changed everything. As president of Picker X-Ray, Harvey was in constant contact with the healthcare system. And Jean had regular stays in hospitals because of a chronic and incurable infection of her neck and head" (Crompton 2006).

In his time immersed in healthcare, Picker found healthcare highly advanced in terms of technology but woefully underperforming in the way it treated patients. This observation intensified with Jean's experiences. As Picker recalled in the *Times* article,

> I am under no illusions that my wife and I were given above-average attention in hospital. But while we were there we saw how other patients' needs were badly neglected. They were left unattended on stretchers in corridors for hours. This was happening all the time in the 1960s and 1970s, in the U.K. as well as America. Now, of course, if it happens it gets far more publicity. Until the middle of the 20th century, if you became ill there were few things we knew how to cure, so patients got very personalised nursing care for almost everything, trying to pull the person through the illness. Then, with penicillin and the introduction of other medical technologies, there was a complete flip. Because you could cure people, personal care became less important and the attitude of healthcare professionals changed from looking at the person to looking at the disease. The pendulum had swung too far the other way (Crompton 2006).

In light of these experiences, Picker and his wife transferred the assets of their small family foundation to The Commonwealth Fund in 1986 and initiated the Picker/Commonwealth Program for Patient-Centered Care, which later became known as the Picker Institute (Kohler 1994). In Picker's words, it was the first body to investigate scientifically not just what patients really wanted from healthcare but also how physicians and healthcare staff could improve the patient experience. Harvey, Jean, and the rest of the team tackled their goal with great vigor and immediately began interviewing patients firsthand.

Over the next seven years, the Picker/Commonwealth program conducted extensive academic research, including more than 8,000 interviews with patients and families, as well as focus groups composed of dozens of caregivers. This research showed that patients' preferences were too often neglected and that amenities, such as hospital food and access to parking, were given far too much significance in existing patient surveys (Kohler 1994).

The Picker Institute developed a wide range of survey tools that quickly set the standard for performance measurement in the healthcare field. In addition to its own research, Picker Institute staff members were part of a large team of investigators from across the country—joining researchers from Harvard Medical School, the Research Triangle Institute, and the RAND Corporation—who worked to develop the Consumer Assessment of Healthcare Providers and Systems (CAHPS) surveys and reports to improve public accountability and support consumer choice. The CAHPS instruments have become the national standard for evaluating care across the country and are now required by the National Committee on Quality Assurance as well as CMS. The Picker Institute's emphasis on standardized instruments and methods of data collection helped support the creation of comparative databases that could facilitate benchmarking and spur quality improvement (Gerteis et al. 1993). As demand for Picker surveys increased, the Institute lacked the capability to run large-scale data collection, processing, and reporting, so in 1994 its survey instruments were acquired by NRC Health (called the National Research Corporation at the time) (Kohler 1994).

The Picker Institute was the first of its kind in that it existed solely to advance the idea of patient-centered care. It argued that what matters most in healthcare is not what physicians or administrators think but what the patient thinks. The bedrock of this argument was the idea that for patients to truly receive the best care possible, they must be involved in the process—and partnership—of care delivery. In short order, the Picker Institute was "considered a leader in promoting patient-friendly medical care" (Hevesi 2008).

This unique approach not only created reams of useful (and at the time rare) patient data but also culminated in a project known as *Through the Patient's Eyes*. This patient-centered masterwork, laid out in a 1993 best seller of the same name (Gerteis et al. 1993), concluded that patients held a high bar in their expectations of a healthcare experience and that the industry had a mountain of work to do to better serve its primary audience.

EIGHT DIMENSIONS OF PATIENT-CENTERED CARE

Out of *Through the Patient's Eyes*, the Picker Institute outlined a plan for health systems and hospitals to improve. From more than eight years of interviews and reams of patient feedback, the Picker team identified eight dimensions of patient-centered care:

1. **Respect for patients' values, preferences, and expressed needs**
   - Respecting the values of each individual patient
   - Involving the patient in medical decisions
   - Treating the patient with dignity
2. **Coordination and integration of care**
   - Clinical care
   - Ancillary and support services
   - Frontline patient care
3. **Information, communication, and education**
   - Accurate information on the patient's clinical condition and prognosis and on the processes of care
   - Additional information to support patient self-care and autonomous patient decisions
4. **Physical comfort**
   - Pain management
   - Assistance with daily activities
   - A supportive hospital environment

5. **Emotional support and alleviation of fear and anxiety**
   - Anxiety over physical treatment and prognosis
   - Anxiety over the impact of the illness on the patient and family
   - Anxiety over the financial effects of illness

6. **Involvement of family and friends**
   - Providing accommodations for family and friends
   - Involving family and close friends in decision making
   - Supporting family members who take on the role of caregiver
   - Recognizing the needs of family and friends, as well as of the patient

7. **Continuity and transition**
   - Providing understandable, detailed information on medications and continuing patient needs
   - Planning and coordinating timely and appropriate treatment and services after discharge
   - Offering continuing information on access to clinical, social, physical, and financial support services

8. **Access to care**
   - Information on the location of needed healthcare services, along with appropriate transportation support
   - Ease in scheduling appointments
   - Accessible specialists and specialty services

These factors proved most important to patients before, during, and after their journey of care. Many of them, such as involvement of family and friends, were novel and underappreciated at the time. "Visitors," as they were often labeled, were not considered a part of the direct care provided to the patient even though their support had an immeasurable impact on the patient's attitude, well-being, and ability to recover. "Continuity and transition" was another underappreciated dynamic. So much of healthcare is episodic; the patient was often expected to transition between care events and locations without much guidance, which proved to be an area of immense frustration and lasting confusion. It was eye-opening for many providers to consider these effects on those they serve. The dimension of emotional support is hugely important to patients and correlates most highly with a patient's recommending an organization to others; however, this aspect of care continues to be a challenge for most organizations.

The Picker Institute's eight dimensions of care aimed to better instruct those who were committed to patient-centered care. It laid out clear, effective techniques for caregivers at every level of healthcare to improve their approach to patients. The project ultimately established a bold mission for healthcare providers across the nation to go forth and find a way to make patient-centered care a reality.

A quarter century has now passed since that landmark study. What has changed in that time?

CURRENT STATE OF PATIENT-CENTERED EFFORTS

Undeniably, activity, resources, and energy have been spent on the mission of patient-centered care. The Picker-inspired movement created vast amounts of patient- and consumer-provided data. Over time, data sets have become faster to collect, easier to access and share, and more robust and meaningful. This data managed to infiltrate healthcare organizations all the way to the top—finally bringing the average patient's evaluation of the care experience to the CEO's desk and the boardroom. Large swaths of organizations have created initiatives to improve the care they deliver. They have broken down siloes that benefited internal departments but not patients. They have tied executive compensation and incentives to patient-provided scores. They have worked hard to uncover patients' preferences beforehand and to follow up after discharge to ensure patients are recovering as planned. The industry has embraced bundled payments as a way to encourage better care, not more expensive care, for patients.

But ask anyone who has had a recent patient experience, and it's clear there hasn't been enough progress. Overall HCAHPS scores increased only about 7 percentage points from 2008 to 2015 (Papanicolas et al. 2017). One of the most dramatic changes in 25 years has been the cost of care. In 2001, the average American family spent about 12 percent of its income on healthcare; now it spends anywhere between 15 and 30 percent, depending on whether the family has employee-sponsored coverage or an individual plan (Kaiser Family Foundation 2019; Sekhar 2009). Most Americans now find themselves unable to comfortably afford healthcare. Medical bills have become a leading cause of personal bankruptcy and divorce. Surprise bills have become the fodder of national media pundits.

What do Americans think about progress? Most consumers are not familiar with healthcare and don't pay much attention to it until they or a family member needs it. When they do access healthcare, they come to it with expectations from other industries—food, hospitality, financial—that they use far more often. Those industries have made leaps and bounds in improving the delivery of a consumer-friendly experience. Healthcare has not, leaving many consumers with a strong desire and incentive to stay away from it—even to their detriment.

Clearly, this widespread perspective would trouble someone like Harvey Picker. Before he passed away in 2008, Picker was still hopeful that healthcare would improve. He often argued that improvement must come from within the rank and file of healthcare organizations themselves—and not only nurses and physicians but senior leaders, too. How and when will healthcare change? Harvey's answer, from a Picker Institute–sponsored Future of Patient-Centered Care Vision Summit in Baltimore in March 2004: "I've never seen an industry change until the fear of remaining the same is greater than the fear of change."

Outside of the hospital tower, it has become evident to consumers that they must own their health. Out of both necessity and stewardship of their own out-of-pocket expenses, consumers have become more aware of healthcare and hungrier for better information and care options. Harvey and Jean Picker saw patient involvement as a key ingredient in advanced patient-centered care. Only recently have healthcare providers begun to encourage their patients to take a more active role in their health. The industry has begun to move from volume-based care to value-based care and from being disease-focused to being health-focused, but much work must still be done and everyone must be involved. It will take a village.

THE ROLE OF TECHNOLOGY

Technology is often pointed to as the salve of the patient experience. Healthcare technology in general has made leaps and bounds since the Pickers' original work. (More details on technological advances are provided in chapter 2.) Even patient-facing technology has changed. The electronic medical record (EMR) didn't exist a quarter century ago; now consumers communicate digitally with medical professionals—or even have virtual healthcare visits—and they have access to more information than anyone ever dreamt possible. The communication is also lightning quick.

But fast and easy is not how consumers would describe healthcare. Although technology has made some improvements, it has not eased the fear, frustration, and outright confusion that many consumers feel during a healthcare experience. In fact, the medical progress we have seen has created more dings and distractions in the patient room. The EMR has caused physicians' eyes to drift away from the patient and toward the screen. Transcription has replaced interaction. Technology in general has caused problems for patients trying to focus on becoming well again.

Technology is a microcosm of all the improvements made in the past quarter century. It has done immeasurable good but also caused immeasurable harm. When it's used to empower the patient and streamline the experience, the results have been impressive. When it's used as a surrogate for real human interaction, it has caused harm. Having ten different apps to manage while trying to figure out an already confusing industry is not exactly progress.

Technology could be considered a new dimension of care, but it cuts across all other dimensions. Having access to care means having access to your own medical history. It means having access to a physician when you want it, including remotely via telehealth in the convenience of your home. Involvement of family and friends means being able to text and tweet at them during your healthcare experience as you would in any other customer transaction.

PICKER'S RELEVANCE TODAY AND IN THE FUTURE

In the midst of all this, one might ask, is the Picker work still relevant today? The crux of this book is to answer that question. So much has changed. Is there any chance those original dimensions of care still hold up? Do patients still value human interaction and efforts to secure their comfort and respect? Research conducted for this book (presented in chapter 6) demonstrates that the dimensions continue to be deeply relevant. For example, emotional support continues to be an important component of patient-centered care, perhaps even more so than it was 25 years ago. Patients still want access to care—they just want it differently today.

Notably, the original Picker work was experience based: Organizations had to prove they boosted their performance. Picker wanted people to transcend measurement and focus on how to actually *improve* their scores. That way, progress could be quantifiably discerned on the basis of internal benchmarks.

Rather than combine existing or third-party data sets, Picker and his team felt it was important to conduct primary research with actual patients—to ask them how their experience was and why they feel the way they do. What is most important to them? And how is that different from the actual experience? What do organizations have to do to bridge any gaps?

This approach was radically different from how healthcare organizations traditionally conducted research. Often because of a C-suite edict, department heads would get together and put the questions they themselves wanted to ask into a questionnaire. Employees and patients would be asked these questions in person. The lack of anonymity and possibility of confrontation often skewed feedback. These internal focus groups were often mere echo chambers. Picker pushed organizations to go beyond their own interests and ask patients directly, "What is important to you?"

After years of success, NRC Health partnered with the Picker Institute in 1994 to expand and further promote the Picker process. NRC Health adopted the Picker dimensions of care and followed the Picker process to conduct direct patient research. Since 2000, NRC Health has received patient feedback regarding 52,988,762 encounters. Through NRC Health's current offerings, the discipline continues to keep the mission to achieve patient-centered care going after all these years.

If Harvey Picker were still alive, what would he say about healthcare today? Contributor Jona Raasch, CEO of The Governance Institute (a service of NRC Health) and former colleague and friend of Harvey Picker, says,

> We are moving way too slowly. Harvey would immediately recognize we are continuing to be challenged by the same issues and problems we dealt with decades ago. Sure, there have been incremental improvements and tweaks to how we approach patients. HCAHPS was a step in the right direction because it forced the issue of patient-centered care throughout the industry and all the way to the top of health system and hospital leadership. But the bottom line is that the progress we have made has come at great cost and slow speed. Harvey may argue we still haven't achieved anything close to the improvements that patients laid out for us in *Through the Patient's Eyes*.

Alas, Harvey and Jean aren't here to tell us what they think. But their legacy endures. They brought focus to an unruly, complex, and massive industry by asking a simple question: In healthcare, who is most important? The answer—as clear as a bell—is the patient. But it is equally clear that this answer has rarely manifested itself in reality. And that's where the Pickers' lifework took aim. *Through the Patient's Eyes* became a call to action for those in healthcare who truly believe the patient is the most important person and that everything must be done with the patient in mind. Harvey and Jean had a dream to transform the healthcare world into a place where caregivers provide effective and compassionate care to everyone and experience joy in their work. That constant striving for improvement is what matters most to patients and consumers; healthcare providers need to continuously learn and seek to better themselves in order to better the patient experience.

NRC Health is striving to continue the Picker legacy. Our mission of human understanding is the next step in the evolution of patient-centered care and a way to carry Harvey's torch. NRC Health's clients are adopting these practices and bringing them to life for their patients. Harvey and Jean Picker would want those improvements to reach as far and wide as possible in the vast industry of healthcare. NRC Health knows that teaching and measuring can go only so far; hospitals and health systems must believe in the work and carry it out every day. Increasingly, that means going outside of the hospital tower or physician's office and delivering human-centered care to wherever humans are. "What Harvey and Jean set out to do was always bigger than any one individual," Raasch shares. "It's always been a collective mission. There were so many insights out of the original work—the dimensions, the 'nothing about me without me' initiative, the push for faster

> What is human understanding? It is the enablement of healthcare organizations to understand what matters most to each person they serve, and to ease that person's journey.

feedback and real-time improvement by moving from research to action. All of those things had to happen on a grand scale, and Harvey always had that vision in his mind."

We will now take a deeper look at where we are today and compare it to where we were 25 years ago—what we've done and what we haven't, and what we've learned and what we still don't know. We will take a close look at how the Picker work still holds up (or doesn't) in today's healthcare age. And what about the future? We will look at what might be happening in healthcare in another 5, 10, or even 25 years.

REFERENCES

Centers for Medicare & Medicaid Services (CMS). 2020. "HCAHPS: Patients' Perspectives of Care Survey." Updated February 11. www.cms.gov/Medicare/Quality-Initiatives-Patient-Assessment-Instruments/HospitalQualityInits/HospitalHCAHPS.

Crompton, S. 2006. "Father of Modern Patient Care." *Times*. Published October 28. www.thetimes.co.uk/article/father-of-modern-patient-care-kfm2qlwg5b3.

Gerteis, M., S. Edgman-Levitan, J. Daley, and T. L. Delbanco (eds.). 1993. *Through the Patient's Eyes: Understanding and Promoting Patient-Centered Care.* San Francisco: Jossey-Bass.

Hevesi, D. 2008. "Harvey Picker, 92, Pioneer in Patient-Centered Care, Is Dead." *New York Times*. Published March 29. www.nytimes.com/2008/03/29/health/29picker.html.

Kaiser Family Foundation. 2019. "The Real Cost of Health Care: Interactive Calculator Estimates Both Direct and Hidden Household Spending." Published February 21. www.kff.org/health-costs/press-release/interactive-calculator-estimates-both-direct-and-hidden-household-spending/.

Kohler, S. 1994. "Case 83: Picker Institute." In *Casebook for the Foundation of a Great American Secret: How Private Wealth Is Changing the World*, edited by J. L. Fleishman, J. S. Kohler, and S. Schindler, 238–39. New York: PublicAffairs.

Papanicolas, I., J. F. Figueroa, E. J. Orav, and A. K. Jha. 2017. "Patient Hospital Experience Improved Modestly, but No Evidence Medicare Incentives Promoted Meaningful Gains." *Health Affairs* 36 (1): 133–40.

Sekhar, S. 2009. "Family Health Spending to Rise Rapidly." Center for American Progress. Published September 15. www.american progress.org/issues/healthcare/news/2009/09/15/6699/ family-health-spending-to-rise-rapidly/.

CHAPTER 2

The Evolution of Patient-Centered Care and Medical Progress

THE PAST FEW decades have seen a lot of activity to improve the patient experience. Numerous factors have influenced this work, including legislative action, healthcare improvement initiatives, and the formation of quality improvement organizations that have helped create ways of quantifying, measuring, and reporting provider performance. Through such efforts focused on improving the quality of care, the healthcare industry has recognized that one key factor must be the patient experience, as it is intricately related to and affects overall quality. In this chapter, we present a brief history of measuring quality and the patient experience, and then describe the relationship between the two.

FOUNDATION OF MEASURING QUALITY

In 1970, the National Academies of Science established the Institute of Medicine (IOM) to help inform the nation on emerging healthcare issues. The IOM has since launched numerous efforts focused on evaluating, informing, and improving the quality of healthcare.

In 1989, the Agency for Health Care Policy and Research was created. This nonprofit organization was renamed the Agency for Healthcare Research and Quality (AHRQ) in 1999, at which time it was reshaped by Congress to exist as the lead federal agency under the umbrella of the US Department of Health and Human Services (HHS) charged with improving the safety and quality of the US healthcare system (AHRQ 2019). This action was in response to newly reported data that revealed wide geographic variations in the use of practices not supported by clinical evidence, as well as growing reports of misuse and overuse of procedural treatments. These findings helped drive congressional prioritization to build a research program focused on investing in clinical effectiveness, treatment outcomes, and practice guidelines (Marjoua and Bozic 2012).

In October 1995, AHRQ launched the first Consumer Assessment of Healthcare Providers and Systems (CAHPS) program, based on the work of the Picker Institute at NRC Health. The initial focus was a multiyear initiative to support and promote the assessment of consumers' healthcare experiences in the hospital inpatient setting. The program now addresses a range of healthcare services to meet the needs of healthcare consumers, purchasers, health plans, providers, and policymakers (AHRQ 2018). The CAHPS program has two main goals:

1. To develop a standardized patient questionnaire to be used to compare results across sponsors and over time

2. To generate tools and resources that sponsors can use to produce understandable and usable comparative information for both consumers and healthcare providers

From 1995 to 2000, several other quality improvement initiatives, task forces, and sentinel reports were initiated and published.

During this time, the IOM published *To Err Is Human: Building a Safer Health System* (1999) and *Crossing the Quality Chasm: A New Health System for the 21st Century* (2001), which addressed quality in a way that patients and consumers could understand. *To Err Is Human* shined a spotlight on the number of deaths due to medical errors in the United States: According to the report, between 44,000 and 98,000 people died in hospitals each year because of preventable medical errors—the equivalent of more than two 747 planes crashing every day for a year. With such statistics, the aviation industry would have been shut down. The report underscored the need for transparency in healthcare and for getting to the root causes of harm. It quantified the costs associated with preventable medical errors and noted that patients were losing trust in physicians and hospitals, emphasizing the diminishing satisfaction of both patients and healthcare professionals.

To Err Is Human created a call to action for all healthcare systems by concluding, "It is not acceptable for patients to be harmed by the healthcare system that is supposed to offer healing and comfort—a system that promises 'First, do no harm.'" The report noted that "this is not a 'bad apple' problem. More commonly, errors are caused by faulty systems, processes, and conditions that lead people to make mistakes or fail to prevent them" (IOM 1999).

Crossing the Quality Chasm went a step further, advocating that Americans should be able to count on receiving care that both meets their needs and is based on scientific knowledge. Although some healthcare organizations were already using evidence-based practices, this approach required a stronger focus throughout healthcare, especially in terms of how care should be delivered and the best ways of practicing medicine. The report illustrated the continued lack of consistent, high-quality medical care. It noted that although medical science and technology were advancing at a rapid pace, the healthcare delivery system was floundering in its ability to consistently provide high-quality care to all Americans. Most disturbing, the IOM noted that since the release of its first report, no real progress had been made on two issues: (1) restructuring healthcare delivery systems to address quality and cost concerns, and (2) advancing information technology to improve administrative and clinical processes (IOM 2001).

Perhaps most importantly, *Crossing the Quality Chasm* introduced the concept of enlisting patients and families as allies in designing, implementing, and evaluating care systems to successfully address the Picker dimensions of patient-centered care and as a fundamental approach to improving the quality of US healthcare (Barry and Edgman-Levitan 2012).

PROGRESS ON ADOPTION OF PATIENT-CENTERED CARE

Further along on the healthcare quality timeline, at the beginning of 2002, the Centers for Medicare & Medicaid Services (CMS) partnered with AHRQ to develop and test the Hospital Consumer Assessment of Healthcare Providers and Systems (HCAHPS) survey—the first national, standardized, publicly reported survey of patients' perspectives on hospital care. The survey instrument comprised 32 items and a data collection methodology for measuring patients' perceptions of their hospital experience. Although many hospitals had collected information on patient satisfaction for internal use, HCAHPS was the first to establish common metrics and national standards for collecting and publicly reporting information about the patient experience of care.

The main goals shaping HCAHPS were (1) to have a standardized survey and implementation protocol and (2) to publicly report the results. Standardization enabled objective and meaningful comparisons between hospitals on the eight dimensions that are most important to patients and consumers. Public reporting of results on the CMS "Hospital Compare" website was the impetus for hospitals to improve their quality of care. It also encouraged a higher level of provider accountability to consumers by increasing the transparency of the quality of care that hospitals provided (CMS 2020).

The AHRQ and its CAHPS Consortium carried out a multi-faceted scientific process in developing the HCAHPS survey. The Centers for Medicare & Medicaid Services provided three opportunities for the public to comment on HCAHPS and responded to more than 1,000 comments. The survey, its methodology, and the results it produces are available to the public on the CMS website (AHRQ 2018).

In December 2005, the National Quality Forum endorsed HCAHPS and the federal Office of Management and Budget gave it final approval for national implementation and public reporting purposes. In October 2006, CMS implemented the HCAHPS survey, and in March 2008, the first set of HCAHPS scores, based on 1.1 million completed surveys, was publicly reported. The number of surveys continued to grow; in 2019, Hospital Compare reported data from 3 million completed surveys. On average, about 8,000 patients complete the HCAHPS survey every day (CMS 2019).

From 2007 to 2016, AHRQ expanded the CAHPS program to other areas beyond hospital care, including physician clinics, home health, hospice, and outpatient and ambulatory surgery. The CAHPS program is still regularly reviewed by CMS to ensure that the survey includes what is most important to consumers.

In 2014, CMS added HCAHPS scores to its Hospital Value-Based Purchasing Program, tying those results to Medicare hospital reimbursements and thus elevating the importance of the CAHPS program. In 2019, the Medicare value-based physician payment system known as the Merit-based Incentive Payment System, which includes clinician and group CAHPS measures in its reimbursement calculations, was fully implemented. The US government's increasing emphasis on value-based payments is largely expected to influence other payers in tying the amount of reimbursement to the patient experience. These moves have placed the improvement of patient experience front and center for healthcare executive and board leadership.

CREATING A MORE CONSUMER-FRIENDLY HEALTHCARE EXPERIENCE

The advent of high-deductible health plans and rising out-of-pocket expenses for consumers have increased awareness of the need for comparison shopping. Consumers want high value when seeking services. To find the best value for their dollar, consumers are starting to search online for physicians, hospitals, and clinics.

Providing consumer-friendly information about health services and price transparency tools can help engage consumers in healthcare before they become hospital patients. However, healthcare provider organizations have only just started to realize the full breadth of information that needs to be captured to effectively create a more consumer-friendly experience. Historically, healthcare providers have done a poor job of listening to their customers. While the government mandate of HCAHPS has provided a basic level of patient satisfaction information, truly listening to the customer involves gathering information about the customer's experience before and after the hospital stay, not just understanding what went wrong in the hospital. Although traditional surveys capture invaluable information about a single care encounter, they don't ask about the experiences that surround it, including booking an appointment, waiting to be seen, and coming to grips with billing and fee structures—all domains that are frustrating to patients and where retail clinics tend to excel.

In fact, approximately 56 percent of patients visit retail clinics because it is much easier to get an appointment with them than with traditional providers (COSHC and IOM 2015). Furthermore, even if they manage to secure an appointment with a physician, almost one-third of patients report unduly long wait times—and 20 percent say they will switch providers if they have to wait too long (Heath 2018). Also, 61 percent of patients find their bills to be confusing, and most of them feel that providers are to blame (Heath 2018).

By zeroing in on what happens in the exam room, many hospitals and health systems neglect opportunities to improve these parallel aspects of their operations. Patient feedback surveys focus on discrete episodes of care, which for most patients are many months or even years apart. As a result, the collection of patient data is inherently sporadic. Nearly half of provider organizations report an inadequate understanding of a patient's journey of care (Gooch 2016).

In 2007, the Institute for Healthcare Improvement (IHI) introduced the Triple Aim as a framework for optimizing health system performance. Underlying this framework is the belief that new care designs must be developed to simultaneously pursue improvements in three dimensions of care:

1. Improve the patient experience (including quality and satisfaction)
2. Improve the health of populations
3. Reduce the per capita cost of healthcare

The Triple Aim placed even greater emphasis on patient-centered care as a central core of high-quality healthcare (IHI 2017).

An important attribute of patient-centered care is the active engagement of patients in making healthcare decisions, because most medical decisions involve more than one reasonable path or option (Barry and Edgman-Levitan 2012). AHRQ's definition of *engagement* includes both activation and engagement: "Patient engagement is the involvement in their own care by individuals (and others they designate to engage on their behalf), with the goal that they make competent, well-informed decisions about their health and healthcare and take action to support those decisions" (AHRQ 2020). Patient engagement is a broader concept than patient satisfaction that combines patient activation with interventions to increase activation and promote positive patient behavior, such as obtaining preventive care or exercising regularly (James 2013). It also involves shared decision-making in which clinicians help patients understand the importance of their values and preferences in making the decisions that are best for them. When patients know they have treatment options, most will want to participate with their clinician in making the best choice (Barry and Edgman-Levitan 2012).

Patient engagement is one strategy to achieve the Triple Aim (James 2013). To facilitate patient activation and engage patients, an organization needs to put patients first and ensure their care is individualized (rather than one-size-fits-all). This means treating the patient as the most important member of the healthcare team and understanding the entire journey through the patient's frame of reference. For example, an individualized approach considers how a patient with a chronic condition would like to communicate after the hospital stay. It may include providing resources such as online communities where patients with that particular condition can discuss their concerns with each other, ask questions of a physician or nurse, and participate in group education by healthcare professionals. It also ensures the healthcare team knows about any barriers the patient is facing that may inhibit compliance with his treatment plan or willingness to engage in healthy behaviors, so that the healthcare team can partner with the individual to achieve the highest quality of life possible.

Ultimately, the heightened focus on healthcare quality and patient experience has helped different stakeholders align around the same essential goals for change, made patients and consumers more aware of the important role they play in managing their own health, and allowed them to see themselves as vital members of the healthcare team. The shifts in attitude have also encouraged patients to expect quality care from all of the organizations they interact with.

Unfortunately, these strides are still not enough. The United States still has large leaps to make before all consumers can receive consistent, high-quality, and patient-centered care in a provider system that is easy to understand and navigate. The healthcare profession needs to stop thinking about patients/consumers only during their times of illness and consider how to interact with them during their times of wellness too. Consumers are demanding change and will go to great lengths to get what they expect from healthcare, whether they find it in a traditional or nontraditional setting.

REFERENCES

Agency for Healthcare Research and Quality (AHRQ). 2020. "Symposium on Patient Engagement (District of Columbia)." Accessed February. https://digital.ahrq.gov/ahrq-funded-projects/symposium-patient-engagement.

———. 2019. "About AHRQ." Published March. www.ahrq.gov/cpi/about/index.html.

———. 2018. "The CAHPS Program." Published October. www.ahrq.gov/cahps/about-cahps/cahps-program/index.html.

Barry, M. J., and S. Edgman-Levitan. 2012. "Shared Decision Making: The Pinnacle of Patient-Centered Care." *New England Journal of Medicine* 366 (9): 780–81.

Centers for Medicare & Medicaid Services (CMS). 2020. "Hospital Compare." Accessed January 6. www.medicare.gov/hospitalcompare/search.html.

———. 2019. "HCAHPS Fact Sheet (CAHPS Hospital Survey)." Published October. www.hcahpsonline.org/globalassets/hcahps/facts/hcahps_fact_sheet_october_2019.pdf.

Committee on Optimizing Scheduling in Health Care (COSHC) and Institute of Medicine (IOM). 2015. "Issues in Access, Scheduling, and Wait Times." In *Transforming Health Care Scheduling and Access: Getting to Now*, edited by G. Kaplan, M. H. Lopez, and J. M. McGinnis, 17–31. Washington, DC: National Academies Press.

Gooch, K. 2016. "61% of Patients Confused by Medical Bills, Survey Finds." *Becker's Hospital Review.* Published July 14. www.beckershospitalreview.com/finance/61-of-patients-confused-by-medical-bills-survey-finds.html.

Heath, S. 2018. "Long Appointment Wait Time a Detriment to High Patient Satisfaction." *PatientEngagementHIT.* Published March 23. https://patientengagementhit.com/news/long-appointment-wait-time-a-detriment-to-high-patient-satisfaction.

Institute for Healthcare Improvement (IHI). 2017. "IHI Triple Aim Initiative." Published June. www.ihi.org/Engage/Initiatives/TripleAim/Pages/default.aspx.

Institute of Medicine (IOM). 2001. *Crossing the Quality Chasm: A New Health System for the 21st Century.* Washington, DC: National Academies Press.

———. 1999. *To Err Is Human: Building a Safer Health System.* Washington, DC: National Academies Press.

James, J. 2013. "Health Policy Brief: Patient Engagement." *Health Affairs.* Published February 14. www.healthaffairs.org/do/10.1377/hpb20130214.898775/full/healthpolicybrief_86.pdf.

Marjoua, Y., and K. J. Bozic. 2012. "Brief History of Quality Movement in U.S. Healthcare." *Current Reviews in Musculoskeletal Medicine* 5 (4): 265–73.

CHAPTER 3

The Rise of the Healthcare Consumer

As MUCH AS patient-centered care has enjoyed the limelight in the past 25 years, healthcare leaders have begun to shift their focus "off campus" to those people who aren't in a gown—yet. Consumers—and the movement of consumerism they represent—have begun to assert their influence on healthcare forcefully. Regular, everyday people now make up the fastest-growing group of healthcare payers in the United States (Daniels 2016). As consumers continue to pay more for healthcare than they have before, they will naturally demand more from healthcare providers. In fact, in any given sector, consumers will ask: If I pay more, do I get more in return? In healthcare, this question weighs heavily on consumers' minds. Faced with skyrocketing out-of-pocket costs and mounting frustration from having little control over their care, consumers are sick of a field meant to keep them well. Armed with vast amounts of information and shrinking patience, consumers aim to change healthcare for the better by standing up for themselves and turning this consumer-challenged industry around. It's no small task.

Consumers have a rising passion to better their health—and their healthcare. Seven in ten consumers feel personally responsible for managing their own health (NRC Health 2016). But very few understand how to navigate the complex system of healthcare choices. Unlike virtually every other sector, consumers lack a working knowledge of their own healthcare. Myriad choices, complicated service flow, lack of upfront price information, and many other factors combine to make healthcare difficult to navigate. Nonetheless, the expectation persists that they can manage these factors on their own.

Consumers' passion is matched by the financial pressure they face. For example, the rise of high-deductible health plans has shifted an immense amount of financial risk from hospitals and insurers to the consumer household—at the same time that consumers are expected to manage their own care successfully and all its responsibilities. Yet we know consumers can struggle to manage their finances, and the complexity of healthcare costs only increases the level of difficulty they face.

As a result, consumers seek meaningful change in healthcare. They seek organizations that understand them and are committed to creating better experiences for families and communities. As consumers continue to be drawn into healthcare decision-making and to play a larger role in their own care, they are less likely to support organizations that they feel are part of the traditional healthcare model. Why pay more for the same old thing? Hunger for innovative and convenient new avenues to care (e.g., urgent care centers, home health, telemedicine) is mostly fueled by a disdain for the current delivery model. Therefore, healthcare providers need to pause and consider the consumer in ways they never have before. Simply attempting to improve the traditional patient experience—which touches very few consumers at any one time—will not impress the new payers of healthcare.

HISTORICAL FACTORS LEADING TO TODAY'S CONSUMERISM MOVEMENT

The rise of the healthcare consumer can feel sudden, but its origins trace back decades. To understand today's consumerism, we must look back at a time when patients began to behave like consumers—the 1970s. Although it wouldn't be formally recognized until much later, the advent of health maintenance organizations began during the decade of disco. This shift was spurred by patients' need to understand the copayments and formulary prescriptions that arose from the structure of managed healthcare. Certain procedures, as determined by the insurance companies, required prior authorization by the healthcare plan before payment to the provider or hospital would be guaranteed. Procedures requiring a prior authorization could be declined, after a review by the health plan for medical necessity, with the full expense then shifting to the insured. Patients often felt caught in the middle, with the physician directing the care and the insurance company determining approval. It was a time fraught with frustration by physicians, who had been accustomed to being paid for the services rendered (fee-for-service) rather than a bundled payment amount. Hospitals and physicians began creating group practices and focusing on delivering outpatient services to counter the impact of reduced reimbursement for patient hospital stays (National Council on Disability 2013).

At the turn of the millennium, laptops, tablets, and smartphones emerged. It would still be years before these devices made any difference in how consumers accessed their healthcare, but behind the scenes, new technologies made electronic medical records (EMR) portable. Documentation could be done literally at the bedside, thus decreasing errors, and EMR systems made information available to multiple clinicians at one time. In hospital patient care areas, computers were often secured on a wheeled table (sometimes called a *cow*); this arrangement allowed transparency, instead of charting taking place later, away from the presence of the patient. The 2000s saw the advent of outcome-based reimbursement, with technological functionality that enabled clinical decision support, analytic solutions, and data warehousing. Most departments still operated in record-keeping silos (e.g., pharmacy medications, clinical care plans, and laboratory orders and results were often on different IT systems). However, EMR adoption was the start of a push for an integrated system to deliver seamless care and provide better communication among all members of the patient's care team (Grandia 2014). It also enabled increasingly safe systems by requiring additional checks before a task could be completed (e.g., medication bar coding, patient ID scanning at the bedside). The national focus on patient safety and adopting processes that augmented clinician performance ran in parallel to much of the work that was being done by the Institute of Medicine to improve quality of care.

From the EMR, computerized systems evolved to the electronic health record (EHR). While the EMR was used predominantly for patient diagnosis and treatment and not designed to be used outside of the hospital or clinical practice, the EHR provided additional benefits to patients and healthcare providers. These included a more complete picture of a patient's overall health, documentation by multiple departments and specialties in the same system, and a platform that promoted healthier lifestyles and more frequent use of preventive care (USF Health 2020). In 2010, only 16 percent of US hospitals were using EHRs. By 2017, 96 percent of hospitals had implemented use of a certified EHR for better documentation of patient outcomes, communication between clinicians, and coordination of care (Office of the National Coordinator for Health Information Technology 2017).

Today, these technological advances have finally found the consumer. Mobile health (*mHealth*, or the viewing of health information on smartphones, tablets, and mobile devices) has enhanced consumers', patients', and healthcare providers' access to, sharing of, and sending of information. The uses of mHealth include placing medical orders, entering clinical documentation, and obtaining greater amounts of information on patients (*Becker's Hospital Review* 2014). The use of secure messaging and encryption has brought greater breadth of private communication. Historically, information was retained within the hospital or clinic walls, sent via fax, or obtained as paper copies by patients, who were required to contact medical records departments. These processes often left consumers feeling frustrated and made healthcare look outdated compared to other industries and experiences.

The use of telehealth has opened a new door to healthcare. Consumers have longed for healthcare to come to them, and they have grown increasingly comfortable with the idea of a virtual visit. This shift is especially true for consumers with difficulty accessing care (e.g., rural consumers). Telehealth has allowed smaller facilities to have access to resources like those available in cities by using technology to communicate. While this is still new to healthcare, initial outcomes seem to indicate that clinics in smaller communities could stay financially afloat and provide 24-hour, 7-day-a-week coverage of the required services. In intensive care units equipped with telehealth devices, mortality rates have been lower and discharge has been 20 percent faster (*Becker's Hospital Review* 2014).

PATIENT USE OF TECHNOLOGY AS AN ACTIVE CARE TEAM MEMBER

The advent of patient portals has allowed consumers and patients to engage with their providers in new and more informed ways. With patient portal technology, patients can log on to an app or a website and access their medical records and interact with their caregivers, all outside of an examination room. This interaction has allowed patients and their families to be more closely involved and better educated in their care (*Becker's Hospital Review* 2014).

Sensors, remote monitoring tools, and wearable technology have also fostered patient involvement. As technology advances, cost shifting has increasingly been placed on employers and consumers through higher premiums, copayments, and deductibles. Patients are also living longer and with more comorbidities. Monitoring patients in their own homes not only provides convenience, but also reduces cost and unnecessary utilization. At the end of 2012, 2.8 million patients worldwide were using a home monitoring device (*Becker's Hospital Review* 2014). In fact, in 2018, the

Centers for Medicare & Medicaid Services (CMS) finalized plans to pay for remote patient monitoring of Medicare patients by home health agencies (Castelucci 2018).

With the use of remote monitoring, healthcare organizations are seeing substantial decreases in hospital readmissions (CMS 2019). The use of sensors and wearable technology has a similar advantage, allowing consumers and patients the freedom and affordability to remain in their homes while ensuring clinical oversight.

After all these advances in the care delivery process, where did the consumer truly enter the picture? By shifting from an EMR to EHR computerized system, care teams brought greater clarity to preventive health and wellness through access to more complete information and a better view of longitudinal care. By taking the long view, care teams began looking at patients differently.

For patients, care went from focusing on a specific encounter to understanding the value of preventive care and wellness—areas well outside of the traditional care experience. The implications were clear: The patient experience needed to be redefined as something more robust. This patient-to-consumer sea change, and the decades-long advancements that powered it, have repositioned patients to be true consumers before they enter a hospital or seek care from a physician and long after the episode of care ends. Today's higher deductibles, copayments, and cost-sharing arrangements have created a powerful responsibility for consumers and their families. The result—and perhaps one of the most significant developments of the past few decades—is that consumers are elevating their role in healthcare and becoming more focused on where, how, and if they elect to seek care.

Consumers are not without resources as they shoulder their new responsibility. With technology at their full disposal, consumers now go online or use apps to obtain pricing information and review online ratings; they use social media to find recommendations from their peers; and they want physician confirmation of information from the internet. Consumers are seeking collaborative relationships, more interaction, and easy-to-access services, not "cookie-cutter" medicine.

This shift in consumer behavior has created new pressures on healthcare workers. Similarly, healthcare organizations are shifting their mindset to one of consumerism, and they are adopting metrics from outside the industry, such as the net promoter score, which looks at the percentage of individuals who promote an organizational brand, to understand the loyalty of their customer base. While patient activation is still important, engaging consumers during all stages of their life cycle becomes paramount in the shift from illness to wellness. A competitor's catchment area is blurring with technology advancements now that consumers can secure medical appointments via their mobile phones for a flat out-of-pocket rate or have a prescription called into the pharmacy for delivery without ever leaving homes. Entrants from fields outside of healthcare have appeared with innovative ways of understanding potential consumers, their buying habits, and their spending patterns. Technology has changed how consumers engage with and access their medical team and information in new ways that will only become heightened in the future.

There is still a long way to go toward consumer-centric care. Perhaps the most important technique that providers can use along the way is engaging the consumer: To design a better relationship with consumers, providers must include their input. If providers build the future of healthcare *for* consumers—but not *by* or *with* consumers—both parties may end up with buyer's remorse.

THE TRIPLE AIM: CONSUMER EDITION

To reshape healthcare through the eyes of the consumer, leaders should start with consumers' core beliefs. No model represents an approach to healthcare in the past three decades like the Triple Aim (as defined in chapter 2: simultaneously improving the patient experience, improving the health of the population, and reducing the per capita cost of care). This concept is the most universally accepted and least controversial in healthcare. Perhaps an even more significant factor is that consumers agree with the importance and focus of the Triple Aim (NRC Health 2012).

The best part of the Triple Aim might not even be its universal acceptance among both providers and consumers, but rather its immediate alignment with many healthcare organizations' current mission and vision. Many hospitals and health systems have recently updated their organizational mission to include the Triple Aim or some version of it.

As much as consumers agree with the Triple Aim, consumers don't speak the language of healthcare. They don't discuss the importance of quality or safety or managing infection rates, and they don't possess much knowledge on how these benchmarks affect their care. Jargon is for insiders, and consumers are healthcare's outsiders. However, in their own language, consumers paint a compelling picture of what they want.

It's time to define the consumer's version of the Triple Aim. Of course, the Triple Aim is important, but we can juxtapose what consumers want with the standard the industry is attempting to achieve. Let's examine the Triple Aim through the consumers' eyes with three consumer-driven issues: access, engagement, and value (see exhibit 3.1).

Consumer Aim 1: Access

To providers, the term *access* may invoke scheduling strategies, physician referral patterns, or capacity challenges. To consumers, access starts much earlier in the care journey and revolves around a central question: How can I find you? It's a question most consumers struggle to answer efficiently. Consumers want to be able to seek out a healthcare organization quickly via their preferred medium. For some consumers, that is still the telephone, but for others it may be a website or an app. Some simply want to walk in

EXHIBIT 3.1: Institute for Healthcare Improvement Triple Aim and Consumer Triple Aim

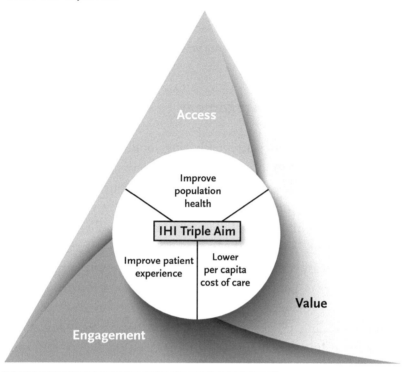

to a provider close to where they work or live. Consumers want to take their first care steps in different ways and don't appreciate a one-size-fits-all approach to access.

Technology has changed the face of medicine, and it continues to accelerate consumer access points. The majority of consumers (74 percent) will access social media websites to find health and healthcare information at some point—often seeking information from additional consumers when they do. A growing number of consumers (27 percent) use a mobile device to find healthcare information and decide where to go. This type of access is not limited to younger generations. The average age of the online healthcare consumer is 45, the same as the average household decision-maker for healthcare services in the United States (NRC Health 2019).

For consumers, it's not as much about healthcare's internal care delivery methodology, but rather their own ability to quickly and easily find their desired care provider. These crucial first steps will define the rest of the consumer and patient care journey, and most often they occur outside the four walls of healthcare facilities.

Consumer Aim 2: Engagement

Long before providers started thinking longitudinally about episodes of care, consumers saw the long view in their own care. For regular, everyday people, healthcare is a journey—a string of episodes lasting months or years that eventually will end. Consumers are hopeful they will "get back to normal" and no longer need healthcare. When consumers are asked about *health* instead, a different story emerges. Consumers don't want engagement solely through a patient experience: They seek guidance beyond the gown. To consumers, health is a container for many personal factors including nutrition, exercise, and overall well-being. To manage and improve their health, they need guidance—but perhaps not in the traditional healthcare way. Consumers don't want healthcare to hijack their own agency to live a healthy life. In fact, seven in ten consumers want to be in control of their health—and their healthcare—but often feel they forfeit much of this control once they enter the world of traditional healthcare. Caregivers must balance their own strategies, processes, and responsibilities against consumers' desire to play a significant role in their own care. True consumer engagement (not simply patient engagement) will involve a significant organizational shift in how consumers' own desires are viewed and valued against healthcare executives' directives.

The difference between consumer engagement and patient engagement is an issue of perception. When we focus on patient engagement, we often turn a blind eye to what happens to our patients before and after they receive treatment. Patient experience pertains to those who are on the receiving end of traditional care—whether experiencing a hospital stay, enduring a surgery, or anxiously awaiting their physician. While these hours or days are essential to all patients and their ultimate health, this time makes up only a small portion of their lives—many perceptions are formed and decisions are made before and after the traditional patient experience. Consumers, on the other hand, are out living their lives long before they become patients. They are working, driving, buying groceries, and generally doing everything but receiving healthcare. Once they sense an issue, they go online, research their options, and speak with similar-minded consumers before they receive any actual treatment.

Further, once consumers are in a gown, they already have formed many perceptions that will influence how they receive care and assess it after the hospital stay or visit to the physician. Consumers will ask themselves: Were my expectations met? They will form opinions about every facet of care they received. They will take stock of their health and their journey to recovery. Engaging patients is vital, but it's only one segment of a vast and winding consumer journey of care. Engaging consumers means healthcare organizations are dedicated to focusing on and caring for people who haven't yet come through the door and following up with them once they have left.

Consumer Aim 3: Value

Once consumers have accessed their care and completed a patient experience, they will calculate value. Value continues to be misunderstood in the context of healthcare. Many executive conversations on value tend to gravitate toward pricing and the cost of care. While affordability is important to consumers, it is only one side of their value equation—a quality experience is on the other side. Quality and cost are the two halves that form a single whole. This yin and yang are often out of alignment for consumers.

For example, if the quality of an experience is poor and the cost is exceedingly high, consumers will feel that the overall experience lacked value. On the flip side, a high-quality experience for a low cost will be considered to be high value. Many healthcare executives get stuck on the issue of cost and ask, Do consumers want the lowest-cost healthcare around? Not necessarily. NRC Health's Market Insights studied consumer perception of cost of care and found that, like other industries, consumers will pay more if they perceive quality to be higher than that of similar products or services. This highlights the need to pair information on outcomes with information on pricing to allow consumers to determine value (NRC Health 2015).

The consumer desire to consider quality alongside cost is intensified by the direction of a particular variable: rising out-of-pocket costs. As with other industries, consumers will ask, If I pay more, what more do I get in return? Because costs have exceeded the rate of inflation and defied common sense, consumers have concluded that the value of healthcare is low. Surprise billing, medical bankruptcies, and massive deductibles have wreaked havoc on wallets. The mounting pressure to pay has forced a large swath of consumers to opt out of healthcare altogether. In 2019, three in ten consumers were deferring necessary medical treatment (NRC Health 2019), a larger group than that in the throes of the Great Recession (27 percent put off care in 2008) (NRC Health 2008). Throughout this astonishing decade of deferment, consumers have consistently said that their main reason for avoidance is the perceived cost of care.

The fear of medical costs is fueled by a crippling lack of transparency in healthcare. Going into an experience, most consumers have no idea what their treatment will cost, leaving them to inflate the figure in their heads, all while quality remains a mystery (see Why Is Quality in Healthcare So Mysterious?).

Healthcare pricing tools have been around for nearly two decades, but very few consumers are aware they exist. Only 13 percent of consumers have visited Hospital Compare in their lifetimes (NRC Health 2015). This is not due to lack of demand; most consumers are actively interested in knowing cost and quality before they become patients. As average deductibles continue to rise, the call for cost and quality transparency will become deafening. Consumers remain largely unconvinced by a growing glut of hospital awards and advertising. They require real evidence to prove that they can not only seek the care they want and need, but that they can afford it, and they would prefer this evidence up front so they can make decisions based on value and follow this assessment throughout their journey of care.

WHY IS QUALITY IN HEALTHCARE SO MYSTERIOUS?

The word *quality* is unfortunately overused in healthcare. The term has become so vague that, if you ask ten healthcare professionals what it means, you will receive ten distinctly different responses. NRC Health's Market Insights sought to understand the word and conducted a test of 23,000 consumers in 2017. This study revealed that consumers also vary greatly in how they define quality. Because there is so little consensus on what quality is and, by extension, so much confusion around how to achieve it, pursuing it can become a trap for providers.

For example, a committee might be put in place to define, measure, and improve quality. The committee members accomplish this by talking with each other and a few clinicians. They come up with a definition that may not be congruent with that of patients or the larger consumer base the organization serves. They don't have an unlimited budget, so they tack a few questions on to an existing survey or they do a small-scale project to measure their newly defined quality against actual patient outcomes. Perhaps they find they are measuring up and they don't make any changes. Perhaps they aren't measuring up, so they reinvest in what they believe will improve quality (often doing more of what they've already been doing—more rounding, more

(continued)

(continued from previous page)

surveys, more coaches, more training, and so forth). They will often chase their tail and find themselves burnt out without much to show. All the while, consumers who demand a personalized experience and define quality differently are left with unmet expectations and subpar experiences. We might do well to come up with a proxy for quality that uses a broader, more consistent interpretation, and measure that proxy against something we can tangibly track and realistically improve. Quality, for many organizations, has been a dream never truly realized.

THE CALL FOR CONSUMER-CENTRIC HEALTHCARE

While the healthcare field's quest for patient-centered care retains immense importance and meaning to those in healthcare, its translation to consumers reveals a different story. Consumers don't necessarily care how we model improvement in the industry; they care that it happens. To them, finding us (access), staying in touch both on and off campus (engagement), and being able to afford us (value) all coalesce into a fairly simple theme, in consumers' own words: "Consider me. Include me. Listen to me. Know that I need you, but also know that I need you to be better. I'm not satisfied with healthcare and neither are you, so let's improve one step at a time, and let's do it together. For healthcare. For everyone."

REFERENCES

Becker's Hospital Review. 2014. "10 Biggest Technological Advancements for Healthcare in the Last Decade." Published January 28. www.beckershospitalreview.com/healthcare-information-technology/10-biggest-technological-advancements-for-healthcare-in-the-last-decade.html.

Castelucci, M. 2018. "CMS Will Pay for Remote Patient Monitoring by Home Health Agencies." *Modern Healthcare*. Published October 31. www.modernhealthcare.com/article/20181031/NEWS/181039966/cms-will-pay-for-remote-patient-monitoring-by-home-health-agencies.

Centers for Medicare & Medicaid Services (CMS). 2019. "Hospital Readmissions Reduction Program (HRRP)." Modified July 31. www.cms.gov/Medicare/Medicare-Fee-for-Service-Payment/AcuteInpatientPPS/Readmissions-Reduction-Program.html.

Daniels, R. S. 2016. *Consumer-Centric Healthcare: 2016 Update*. Chicago: William Blair.

Grandia, L. 2014. "Healthcare Information Systems: A Look at the Past, Present, and Future." Health Catalyst. Published May 20. www.healthcatalyst.com/insights/healthcare-information-systems-past-present-future.

National Council on Disability. 2013. "Appendix B. A Brief History of Managed Care." In *Medicaid Managed Care for People with Disabilities: Policy and Implementation Considerations for State and Federal Policymakers*, 161–64. Published March 18. https://ncd.gov/publications/2013/20130315/20130513_AppendixB.

NRC Health. 2008, 2012, 2015, 2016, 2017, 2019. *Market Insights Surveys*. Lincoln, NE: NRC Health.

Office of the National Coordinator for Health Information Technology. 2017. "Non-federal Acute Care Hospital Electronic Health Record Adoption." Health IT Quick-Stat 47. Published September. https://dashboard.healthit.gov/quickstats/pages/FIG-Hospital-EHR-Adoption.php.

USF Health. 2020. "Differences Between EHR and EMR." Accessed January 10. www.usfhealthonline.com/resources/key-concepts/ehr-vs-emr.

CHAPTER 4

Building a Consumer–Provider Relationship

Now that we have chronicled the rise of the healthcare consumer, we can see why the industry must adapt to a shifting, consumer-driven landscape. Consumers have laid out their needs, and providers must be prepared to deliver. If they don't, they risk alienating their future patients, the ultimate determinants of their success or failure. In response to this pressure, can't consumer-minded providers simply start crafting relationships with their own patients? Can't they reach out and engage these consumers somehow? As is true in much of healthcare, it's not that simple. Many barriers, each formidable in different but not entirely dissimilar ways, stand firmly between the provider and the consumer.

SIX DEGREES OF SEPARATION

Perhaps you recall the fame game of the 1990s, "Six Degrees of Kevin Bacon." The game informally posited that every human on the planet is only six people away from knowing the famed *Footloose* actor. Bacon was the friend of a friend of a friend of a friend, if you will. Think of Kevin Bacon as a proxy for our healthcare consumer. In extensive, decades-long research, NRC Health's Market

Insights (a panel of consumers providing feedback on healthcare) has identified six distinct barriers that often keep providers and consumers from engaging and establishing meaningful relationships. For providers, the six degrees of separation are strategic and operational gaps. Understanding what they are and why they keep consumers away is the first step toward realizing a true consumer–provider relationship.

Degree of Separation 1: An Industry Ignored

Separation between consumer and provider often begins in the mind. NRC Health's research reveals a universal truth: Consumer perceptions create market realities. Many paradoxes characterize how consumers think about healthcare. Consumers generally avoid thinking about healthcare and often do not consider it a high priority in their lives until a health issue emerges. Healthcare then becomes their top, and often only, priority until the issue is resolved. Yet, as much as consumers usually keep their present and future healthcare needs at the back of their mind, a general sentiment about the industry creeps to the center: Healthcare is broken. NRC Health's Market Insights surveys have revealed that while most consumers don't actively think about healthcare, they do have strong opinions about it. In general, they feel that healthcare needs a serious overhaul, though they are unable to describe exactly how they want such reform to unfold. Many consumers admit they simply don't know enough about healthcare—and don't even realize how little they know—until they are thrust into a medical situation.

This much is clear: The intersection between healthcare consumers' limited knowledge and their negative sentiments toward the industry undergirds the journey of care and begins long before health issues surface. This unintuitive blend of emotion and knowledge (or lack thereof) ensures that most consumers set off on the wrong foot, and it explains why the care journey is plagued with confusion and a lack of confidence as individuals try to navigate an industry that seems out of focus—made worse by the dark cloud hanging over it all.

Consumer confusion and lack of understanding are exacerbated by the lack of outreach *to* consumers *by* providers. Healthcare organizations tend to understaff their marketing departments and often rely on antiquated methods of advertising (Greystone.Net and Klein & Partners 2016). For example, a healthcare marketer may continue to place outdoor advertisements because an influential physician demands to see his face on a billboard as he drives into his practice. A healthcare business development executive might run into the boardroom sentiment that hospitals really don't (or shouldn't) need to compete for patients, a position that doesn't align with the competitive realities of healthcare. These stubborn notions create an environment in which consumer engagement gets bogged down or mothballed entirely by provider politics. In his book, *Joe Public Doesn't Care About Your Hospital*, healthcare marketing expert Chris Bevolo (2011) explains, "So much of what hits the streets by way of marketing initiatives, especially advertising campaigns, is driven not by sound marketing strategy but in response to internal political pressure."

NRC Health has been testing advertising efforts by healthcare organizations, in both quantitative and qualitative settings, for more than a decade. During that time, insights point to an industry filled with healthcare brands struggling to define themselves. Nearly every healthcare organization's advertisements attempt to convey their compassion *and* advanced technology, while also talking up their physicians, slipping in their latest awards, and layering classical music over the top with a splash of blue or green in the logo. This bland approach adds confusion to consumers' already loose grasp of their healthcare options. Even as captive audience members in a research setting, consumers struggle to assign the correct brand name to recently viewed ads. Many of these ads fail to break through in consumers' minds, which are already barraged by thousands of ads every day. This leaves people with "brand blur" and little ability to distinguish between providers for care in the future (NRC Health 2019). When we don't consider the consumer, they don't consider us. This lack of understanding in healthcare is a two-way street.

Degree of Separation 2: The Bright Light

What could cause consumers to know little about healthcare but feel the industry needs to change? The "healthcare is broken" narrative has been written by many authors, but perhaps none with a stronger pen than the national and local media. In the never-ending quest for eyes and ears, journalists have had a field day parading healthcare's deficiencies to consumers.

This bright light is never more searing than when the topic turns to the rising costs of care. The belief that healthcare costs have careened out of control—and providers are largely to blame—remains a media focus. According to Harvard economist David Cutler, the number one reason our healthcare costs are so high is that "the administrative costs of running our healthcare system are astronomical . . . far higher than [those of] any other country" (Epstein 2019). Another reason cited is that hospitals are able to sustain profits and high prices because of their market power (Gee 2019). It's hard to fathom any industry's billing process being breaking news, but hospital bills are often front-page fodder and gripping national news narratives (Terhune 2018). What consumers must pay, down to the line item, became the topic of a popular *Time* magazine article by Steven Brill (2013) titled "A Bitter Pill," as well as a *New York Times* bestseller, *America's Bitter Pill* (Brill 2015). Brill wrote of how industry pricing models are set up to benefit virtually all care stakeholders—from pharma to health plans to physicians—at the expense of the patient. It's a searing narrative against hospitals, and it doesn't end there. Industry-roiling scandals such as the EpiPen price gouge, the Ebola public relations fiasco in Texas, and whatever might hit the news next week have all given everyday consumers plenty of reason to believe healthcare is a harsh and even corrupt world.

This negative coverage is missing a response from the healthcare industry. Sure, the American Hospital Association might issue a press release and local providers may push back via an employee memo or their social media feeds, but often there is no substantial counternarrative in the media from healthcare organizations. Do we simply hope consumers are wearing earmuffs? We know, through research, that consumers are listening, and healthcare organizations would be wise to issue an appropriate response. A counternarrative and swift consumer-facing response is standard in other industries.

For example, consider JetBlue's week-long operational breakdown in 2007. The East Coast–based airline saw its operations collapse during an ice storm that forced it to cancel more than 1,000 flights over five days. CEO David Neeleman could have taken the easy way out and hid behind the legitimate excuse of bad weather. Instead, he wrote a public letter of apology to JetBlue's customers, introduced a customer's bill of rights, and presented a detailed list of what the company would do to help affected passengers, including monetary compensation (Bhasin 2011). It wasn't easy to mollify those affected but, in the weeks following the crisis, JetBlue managed to mitigate much of the public backlash by being straightforward and telling its story. Neeleman went on *CNN*, *Today*, and the *Late Show with David Letterman*, and he even posted videos on YouTube apologizing for letting passengers down. JetBlue kept its sterling reputation intact, which would not have happened had the company not told its story to the most important audience: consumers.

Public relations success stories such as these are commonplace in most industries, except healthcare. When healthcare organizations don't respond to negative publicity, consumers don't hear the full story and cannot make an informed judgment. To bridge this informational gap, providers must be willing to tell their side of the story to the media.

Degree of Separation 3: Follow the Money

Not surprisingly, the most negative narratives on healthcare have revolved around cost. It's too big to miss. Healthcare spending was 18 percent of America's gross domestic product in 2019, triple what it was 50 years earlier (Statista 2019). It's hard not to notice when one of every five US dollars is spent on a single industry, especially when more of those dollars are coming out of the wallets and purses of consumers via sky-high deductibles and rising insurance premiums—money flowing to an industry they often ignore and largely try to avoid.

In a typical calendar year, consumers' first exposure to healthcare is often defined by a lack of affordability. For the 156 million commercially insured individuals in the United States (Berchick, Hood, and Barnett 2018), their "year of healthcare" begins with the open-enrollment period. Unfortunately, for many people, the only choice is between high-deductible and *higher*-deductible plans. Given the nearly unfathomable reality of individual and family deductibles ranging from $6,000 to more than $10,000, it makes sense that consumers are responding by deferring healthcare (as discussed in chapter 3) because they simply cannot afford it.

When care is essential, cost remains top of mind. Seven in ten consumers believe that cost will make a difference in where they'll go for care in the future (NRC Health 2015). As we discussed in chapter 3, in consumers' search for value, their attempts to find cost and quality information remain frustrating. It is most maddening to high-deductible consumers, who search longer and more often for healthcare pricing than consumers with lower deductibles. Seventy-four percent of high-deductible consumers have searched for pricing information (NRC Health 2015), but the resources simply aren't there yet. Vital pricing information is not readily available to consumers, and providers have been slow to step in and help.

As more consumers enter the high-deductible arena and pay for their own care, the frustration with price opaqueness will only grow, and providers will face increasingly agitated consumers. As famed US economist Milton Friedman (2004) laid out in his "four ways to spend money" theorem, we spend other people's money differently from how we spend our own. Gone are the days of $100 deductibles. The role of consumer as payer is distinctly different from the role of consumer as patient. The pain of paying for healthcare may be preventing individuals from receiving the care they need. It also keeps them from building a good relationship with those who provide their care.

Degree of Separation 4: Infinite Information

In today's age of ubiquitous digital information and more screens than US citizens, consumers have an incredible wealth of information at their fingertips. Google gave consumers instant access to libraries of information. Facebook gave consumers the ability to instantly share information within their own social networks. Mobile technologies, chiefly smartphones, gave consumers the ability to participate in these activities virtually anytime and anywhere.

These trends cut across all consumer demographics. Nearly nine in ten consumers go online daily (Pew Research Center 2019). Three in four use social media regularly; one in three can recall visiting a hospital website; one in five have used social media for healthcare purposes; three in ten use a mobile app for healthcare information; and 35 percent use a wearable device every day for health-related purposes (NRC Health 2019). It's not just millennials—older Americans are increasingly going online for health information (NRC Health 2019). In fact, the average age of consumers who use social media to obtain healthcare information is now 44 years old (NRC Health 2015).

What about their level of trust in the information they find? Consumers trust social media five times more than they do advertisements (NRC Health 2015). Fifty-two percent are likely to prefer a healthcare brand after engaging in a positive online interaction. For consumers, these interactions are a modern version of the house call. The days of consumers having to travel to an appointment may be waning, as technology enables providers to bring the experience to the consumer. This out-of-hospital approach could convert our information age from a barrier to a bridge.

Degree of Separation 5: Greener Grass

Consumers' expectations for healthcare are higher than those for any other industry (see exhibit 4.1). Getting 82 percent of Americans to agree on much of anything is difficult, but when it comes to healthcare, the response is nearly unanimous: Consumers want their expectations met or exceeded, or they may walk away dissatisfied. Why the high bar for healthcare? Rising out-of-pocket costs have raised consumer expectations faster than those for other industries. Also, healthcare is different in that its main purpose is

EXHIBIT 4.1: Industries That Should Meet or Exceed Consumer Expectations

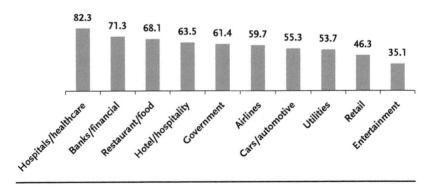

Which of the following industries *should* consistently meet or exceed your expectations as a customer?

Source: NRC Health (2015).

to save lives—not many industries can claim that level of importance. The fact that healthcare can be a matter of life or death tends to propel expectations even higher.

Another factor boosting consumer expectations in healthcare, which may be more difficult for providers to see, is what consumers do outside of healthcare delivery. The average consumer lives most of her life without wearing a hospital gown—buying groceries, eating out, traveling, and so forth. She consumes many more non–healthcare-related services than healthcare-related services. As such, consumers engage in service industries on a day-to-day basis in ways that they have come to expect everywhere. Uber delivers rides in minutes, Southwest Airlines gives points to incentivize repeat travel, and Apple provides consumers with access to experts at a Genius Bar. These positive experiences become instilled in consumers who then expect access, engagement, and value that, as we established in chapter 3, they rarely realize in healthcare.

Many healthcare organizations have shielded their offerings from comparisons with other industries, such as banking, airlines, and food services. The defenses are plenty: Healthcare is more regulated than other industries, healthcare faces limitations because of its responsibility to protect patient health information, healthcare isn't something you just order up, or perhaps that healthcare is simply different. This defensiveness blocks us from comparing ourselves with other industries and learning how our patients determine their expectations. For consumers, healthcare should not only measure up to other service industries, it should surpass them. And consumers would ask any healthcare provider whose chief concern is with the patient experience: How do you hope to provide an experience that meets my expectations if you don't know what they are?

Healthcare hasn't much hope of meeting consumer expectations if it can't learn from other industries along the way. Here is a look at three nonhealthcare companies and what they have done to meet—and exceed—consumer expectations.

Hospitality: Hilton Introduces the Digital Key

While expectations typically aren't as high as in healthcare, hospitality is an industry that faces heavy competition among established brands such as Marriott and Hilton as well as from start-ups like Airbnb. A growing number of travelers demand a perfect experience from their hotels and are willing to pay more per room to satisfy these demands (Sheinman 2018). Parallels exist between hotel and healthcare brands with respect to how consumers want to access and engage these industries.

Hilton Hotels is in the thick of the competition to be the preferred destination for travelers, but not much has changed in their arrival experience. Every traveler fears the long, slow-moving line to check in to the hotel. Even shortcut lines for rewards members can slog along. Everyone in line has a reservation—they just need their room key. Hilton decided to give its guests a way to bypass the line by using a digital key. This technology allows a hotel room to be unlocked by a guest's smartphone—no plastic key or 30-minute wait in line required (Grosvenor Technology 2017). Changing door entry systems and building app-based technology that could consistently deliver such a special experience entailed a significant investment by Hilton. But the bet Hilton is making isn't a technology bet, it's an access bet. Skipping the line and going straight to their room allows guests to get where they want to go faster. It also works within the Hilton app, which behooves travelers to join the Hilton Honors rewards program if they haven't already. Consistent access can lead to increased loyalty over time.

Entertainment: Blockbuster Is Bested by Cost and Convenience

Virtually all consumers have ditched one diversion from the past: a trip to the video store. In its heyday, Blockbuster was the king of entertainment: a $5 billion company that boasted more than 9,000 stores in 2004 (Harress 2013). What Blockbuster perhaps never realized was the dissatisfaction consumers experienced in crowded stores with sold-out movies and no employees in sight.

Then there was the other rite of passage: speeding back to the store at 11:59 p.m. the next night to avoid the dreaded late fee. Remember rewind fees? It turns out the movie rental experience wasn't so rosy. But what choice did consumers have? Blockbuster knew there wasn't much of an alternative, so the idea of disrupting its own success seemed unnecessary. This practice happens in healthcare all the time.

However, just a few years after Blockbuster's peak, two upstarts arrived that would completely change how consumers enjoyed their entertainment: Netflix and Red Box. Their models were different: Netflix offered convenience by sending movies to members via the mail, while Redbox hung its hat on price, offering $1 movies at kiosks. But business was still good for Blockbuster, so for a few years the company didn't do much, while Netflix and Red Box grew impressively (Wilson and Crawford 2011).

Blockbuster then found itself in a dogfight trying to fend off its competitors. It had hung on to its traditional model and was way behind in offering mail rentals and kiosks. The company never anticipated how quickly consumers would leave behind the routine of renting movies to make the experience more convenient.

Retail: Amazon Evolves from Bookseller to Go-To Source for Everything

Who would buy diapers from a bookseller? That's exactly what today's consumers do, and their favorite source is Amazon.com. Long before it boasted 100 million subscribers to its Prime membership service (Green 2019), Amazon started as an online bookseller competing with Barnes & Noble and a host of other physical bookstores. Amazon's virtual store advantage slowly attracted more and more customers as consumers opted to have their literary entertainment delivered to their door instead of visiting brick-and-mortar storefronts. The virtual bookstore bet worked, and most of Amazon's competition has since gone out of business.

Amazon has transcended the bookstore scene and now offers a website full of almost every product imaginable, all available within two days via Prime. It's not just about being fast and easy. Amazon's customers enjoy the ability to instantly calculate value. While searching for products and scanning their options, consumers can sort on the basis of price, composite reviews from consumers who bought the product, and similar products with similar prices and ratings. Gone are the days of asking a family member or neighbor about a product when you can consult hundreds of previous buyers and read their feedback boiled down to a single rating on a five-star scale.

Any way you slice it, consumers appreciate the full transparency that Amazon delivers—so much so that they will pay more to be members of Prime than they will the alternative memberships offered by big box retailers. Consumers decided a while back that value is more about finding the product that fits their needs in terms of quality and cost than it is about doing what they have done in the past. Amazon and other innovators have won big by rejecting existing business models to deliver what consumers want.

No industry is exactly like healthcare, but when studying consumers, looking at their behavior outside of healthcare is important. Every other industry seems to have faced a consumer-led revolution, from banks wrestling with the ATM versus teller issue in the 1980s and 1990s, to airlines adjusting to the transparency of online travel booking sites in the 2000s, to Kodak inventing the portable digital camera but continuing to invest in its film business until its bankruptcy in 2012 (Dan 2012). What cuts across industries is the idea that those who listen to the consumer tend to know where things are going next, and those who cling to existing business models tend to get left behind.

As more and more consumers are wowed by other industries, the pressure on healthcare brands will only be ratcheted up. Even those few healthcare brands that consistently deliver an exceptional experience need to realize that there is pressure to *continue* to exceed consumer expectations. Those expectations are rising and, unless the cost of care goes down, they will continue to climb for some time. Meeting high expectations isn't easy, but the alternative is to risk not existing anymore.

THE INVASIVE SPECIES OF HEALTHCARE

Not all healthcare competition is coming from the world of e-commerce or Silicon Valley. Very real threats exist in every community in the form of retail chain giants that already possess quasi-healthcare brands. An NRC Health Market Insights survey asked consumers to consider receiving care in physical retail locations outside their current patterns of care. In some cases, the scenario was hypothetical only. The results were fascinating. Two brands that begin with "Wal" performed quite well across the country. When consumers were asked if they would go to a retail location for preventive or routine care services (e.g., a flu shot), 48 percent said they would go to Walgreens and 51 percent said they would go to Walmart. For a more serious test or procedure (e.g., magnetic resonance imaging), the results were even more intriguing. Forty percent of consumers said they would go to Walgreens and 38 percent said they would go to Walmart. Walmart doesn't even own such services, but when pressed on why they would consider a retail giant outside of traditional healthcare options, consumers were clear: Walmart would be more affordable and convenient. This response may shock some providers, but it shouldn't; consumers are hungry for something different. It's why they flocked to urgent care two decades ago and why there are now more than 2,000 such clinics in the United States. If consumers don't know the value of their local healthcare providers, they will consider other options. And if those options happen to be well-known brands that offer them convenience and perceived value, consumers just might choose them (NRC Health 2015).

Degree of Separation 6: The Rise of Choice

Our first degree of separation focused on the minds of consumers and their lack of knowledge about healthcare while being tasked with the responsibility to navigate the system on their own. This last degree of separation brings us full circle: the barriers in the minds of healthcare providers.

Healthcare has spent as much time dismissing consumerism as it has trying to adapt to it. Time and again, healthcare leaders ask, Do consumers really have a choice? Don't they listen to their physicians or just follow their networks? Speaking of networks, shouldn't we consider health plans our customers? Questions such as these were more valid in the days of $100 deductibles. Consumers are now paying more than ever before and asking, What have you done to be better than before? Why are you valuable enough for me to be your patient? Unfortunately, many providers struggle to answer these questions. Fewer than half of hospitals in the United States conduct consumer research other than administration of the Hospital Consumer Assessment of Healthcare Providers and Systems (HCAHPS) survey (NRC Health 2019). Even though reporting is mandated, it took until 2015 (nine years after fielding began) for a majority of hospital boards to report that they reviewed HCAHPS information at least once a year (Peisert 2015). Even when the data are in front of us, it can still be too easy for healthcare organizations to tune out the consumer in favor of more insular priorities.

On the other hand, we know consumers also can tune out providers. When they do pay attention to healthcare, plenty of tools are available to them. Yet, even though consumers can go online and find answers, the information typically isn't sufficient, and it isn't from their own healthcare providers.

When consumers don't have a ready go-to source, they often choose a do-it-yourself approach. As we know, they can opt out of healthcare services in favor of an alternative route to health and well-being. Recall that seven in ten consumers want control of their care journey, and that journey often starts with health. The health and wellness industry has grown immensely in the past decade, and consumers' openness to receiving wellness information has also grown. An NRC Health Market Insights survey found that if a hospital or health system hosted a wellness event to engage consumers, 43 percent would like to attend. Further, more than half of consumers (52 percent) would submit to a health risk assessment or other screening if they could receive a readout of their results (NRC Health 2015). Individuals are hungry for wellness education, preferring cooking classes and fitness training to online healthcare articles or health trackers alone. However, there are limitations to do-it-yourself health, and consumers can't—and shouldn't—go it alone. The United States is wrestling with what happens when consumers don't have the guidance they need: the opioid crisis, childhood obesity epidemic, and prevalence of diabetes and prediabetes across the population. Consumers can't do it alone—so who will help them?

Consumer activation is contingent on the behavior of healthcare providers. If providers continue to ignore or underplay consumerism, then consumers will remain information rich and knowledge poor, unable to realize their full potential and frustrated by the reality of having less control and self-confidence than they had hoped for in their care journey. Consumers need someone they can trust to help them make sense of the healthcare information they have—someone who is invested in them, in their community, and in their future. Despite the appeal of digital offerings, the reality still comes down to flesh-and-blood providers stepping up and respecting the consumer's point of view, and the idea that consumers do in fact have some choice in where they go for healthcare services. Without this respect, it is hard to imagine any healthcare provider's offerings truly connecting with consumers.

THE DANGER OF THINKING LIKE A CONSUMER

Once we begin to consider the consumer's point of view, it can be easy to insert yourself or your family members and friends as proxies for consumers in your area. Your experiences and those of people around you can give rise to sweeping notions of who consumers are and what they want. If you are in a healthcare profession, pause before you try to walk in the shoes of a consumer. You know much more about how healthcare works than the average person. If you talk about "continuum of care" or debate "meaningful use," you're too close to the fire and too far from consumers.

This proxy approach is well meaning but can end badly. For example, a CEO may feel that she knows local healthcare and decides not to conduct any research directly with consumers. Or a vice president of marketing may conduct a survey but his own biases and assumptions end up distorting the data collected. When someone in healthcare tells a story of her own experience as a patient, she may even say something along these lines: Thank goodness I had someone at the hospital I could call. That is a warning sign because the average consumer has no one to call. Even when our intentions are good, we really can't understand consumers without asking them. There is no substitute.

REFERENCES

Berchick, E. R., E. Hood, and J. C. Barnett. 2018. *Health Insurance Coverage in the United States: 2017.* Published September. www.census.gov/content/dam/Census/library/publications/2018/demo/p60-264.pdf.

Bevolo, C. 2011. *Joe Public Doesn't Care About Your Hospital.* Nashville, TN: RockBench Publishing.

Bhasin, K. 2011. "9 PR Fiascos That Were Handled Brilliantly by Management." *Business Insider.* Published May 26. www.businessinsider.com/pr-disasters-crisis-management-2011-5.

Brill, S. 2015. *America's Bitter Pill: Money, Politics, Backroom Deals, and the Fight to Fix Our Broken Healthcare System.* New York: Random House.

———. 2013. "A Bitter Pill: Why Medical Bills Are Killing Us." *Time.* Published April 4. https://time.com/198/bitter-pill-why-medical-bills-are-killing-us/.

Dan, A. 2012. "Kodak Failed by Asking the Wrong Marketing Question." *Forbes.* Published January 23. www.forbes.com/sites/avidan/2012/01/23/kodak-failed-by-asking-the-wrong-marketing-question/.

Epstein, L. 2019. "6 Reasons Healthcare Is So Expensive in the U.S." *Investopedia.* Updated July 30. www.investopedia.com/articles/personal-finance/080615/6-reasons-healthcare-so-expensive-us.asp.

Friedman, M. 2004. "Liberty Quotation: Milton Friedman on the Four Ways to Spend Money." Libertarian Party of Maryland. Published July 9. https://lpmaryland.org/liberty-quotation-milton-friedman-four-ways-spend-money/.

Gee, E. 2019. "The High Price of Hospital Care." Center for American Progress. Published June 26. www.americanprogress.org/issues/healthcare/reports/2019/06/26/471464/high-price-hospital-care/.

Green, D. 2019. "A Survey Found That Amazon Prime Membership Is Soaring to New Heights—but One Trend Should Worry the Company." *Business Insider.* Published January 17. https://markets.businessinsider.com/news/stocks/amazon-more-than-100-million-prime-members-us-survey-2019-1-1027877518.

Greystone.Net and Klein & Partners. 2016. *The State of Digital Marketing in Healthcare Moving Toward 2017.* Published November. www.greystone.net/docs/default-source/surveys/the-state-of-digital-marketing-in-healthcare-in-2017.pdf.

Grosvenor Technology. 2017. "Knock, Knock, Knocking on Hilton's Door." Published August 11. www.grosvenortechnology.com/2017/08/knock-knock-knocking-hiltons-door/.

Harress, C. 2013. "The Sad End of Blockbuster Video." *International Business Times.* Published December 5. www.ibtimes.com/sad-end-blockbuster-video-onetime-5-billion-company-being-liquidated-competition-1496962.

NRC Health. 2015, 2019. *Market Insights Surveys.* Lincoln, NE: NRC Health.

Peisert, K. C. 2015. *21st Century Care Delivery: Governing in the New Healthcare Industry.* Biennial survey report. Lincoln, NE: The Governance Institute.

Pew Research Center. 2019. "Internet/Broadband Fact Sheet." Published June 12. www.pewinternet.org/fact-sheet/internet-broadband/.

Sheinman, A. J. 2018. "Hotel and Air Prices to Rise Sharply in 2019, per GBTA/CWT Research." *Meetings & Conventions.* Published July 24. www.meetings-conventions.com/News/Breaking-News/Hotel-and-Air-Prices-to-Rise-Sharply-in-2019,-Per-GBTA/CWT-Research/.

Statista. 2019. "U.S. National Health Expenditure as Percent of GDP from 1960 to 2019." Accessed February 1, 2020. www.statista.com/statistics/184968/us-health-expenditure-as-percent-of-gdp-since-1960/.

Terhune, C. 2018. "Life-Threatening Heart Attack Leaves Teacher with $108,951 Bill." National Public Radio. Published August 27.

www.npr.org/sections/health-shots/2018/08/27/640891882/
life-threatening-heart-attack-leaves-teacher-with-108-951-bill.

Wilson, T. V., and S. Crawford. 2011. "How Netflix Works." How
Stuff Works. Accessed March 3, 2020. https://electronics.
howstuffworks.com/netflix5.htm.

CHAPTER 5

Organization, Culture, and Leadership

We have now established that consumer expectations for healthcare are incredibly high. We also know that the barriers to meeting these expectations are quite formidable. To have any hope of meeting those expectations, we must turn toward our greatest resource: the leaders and doers within the field. We need to ask ourselves point blank: Are we up for the challenge? Can we make it through the gauntlet of consumer and patient expectations laid down for us? We need to take stock in who we are before we get caught up in what we must do.

CHOOSING HEALTHCARE

Healthcare is a calling. Talk to just about anyone in the field and they will say they specifically chose this industry to make a difference in the world. It is rare to find an industry so central to everyone's existence. We lose sight of how healthcare is woven into the fabric of our being. Most of us were born in a hospital, and many of us will die in one. Healthcare guides us from the cradle to the grave and during many of our most important moments in between. We rely on nurses and physicians during our most vulnerable and memorable life events. Inside the world of healthcare, infants are born, heights are checked off, and life is lived from beginning to end.

People drawn to healthcare desire to make the world a better place. Physicians aren't the only ones who ascribe to the Hippocratic oath: first, do no harm. We all want to make people better. And we all know healthcare isn't perfect, so we want to make it better, for patients and for ourselves. The question is this: As an industry and as a people, how do we get there?

As the previous chapters have laid out, the challenge is massive. It is fair to question whether progress has truly been made in advancing to patient-centered healthcare. Many patients still feel let down and describe an industry that is falling short of expectations. Scores on the Hospital Consumer Assessment of Healthcare Providers and Systems (HCAHPS) survey have not led to improved care and experience to the degree originally hoped a decade ago. The cost of healthcare has spiraled out of control, even with heavy investment in value-based purchasing.

MEASUREMENT OVERLOAD

While many have expressed doubt about improvement in healthcare, there is little dissent in one area that has seen a remarkable activity spike in the past decade: measurement. We have measured ourselves to the nth degree. If we could be flies on the wall of healthcare organizations, we'd have heard *measurement* a million times. The term has been bandied about in board meetings, at executive retreats, and among employees. Entire businesses have been erected to focus on measuring the patient and consumer experience. In fact, an entire "culture of measurement" has been created in nearly every corner of the field.

Although there is consensus that we measure much more of the patient experience than we did in the time of Harvey and Jean Picker, there is also much debate about what all that measurement has taught us (see exhibit 5.1). For example, a big focus of HCAHPS

EXHIBIT 5.1: The System Is Designed to Deliver Metrics, Not Better Experiences

Percentages of patients reporting a positive overall experience for all hospitals and hospitals in the Value-Based Purchasing (VBP) program, 2008–14

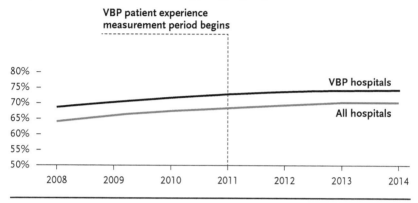

Source: Papanicolas et al. (2017). Reprinted with permission.

was to shrink the large number of patients who were not willing to recommend a hospital after a care experience. In 2008, at the outset of HCAHPS public reporting, 33 percent of patients across the United States did not recommend a hospital (NRC Health 2008). In 2016, after eight years of HCAHPS measurement and more than $1 billion spent on improvement, 28 percent of patients were not willing to recommend a hospital after a care experience (NRC Health 2016). Considering the money and effort spent, we do not consider this reduction to be a victory.

In defense of measurement, it is impossible to know if an industry has changed—especially one as complex as healthcare—without systematic and widespread gathering of information. Evidence is especially important in an industry in which memories are long and anecdotes abound. To prove things have changed in healthcare, every organization has to ponder, devise, and deploy an intensive measurement program that covers all facets of care across the organization and digs into enough detail to yield meaningful insights. The complex experiences within the ecosystem of healthcare require it. But we argue that healthcare has now reached a point where our next challenge is to determine how to measure what truly matters most.

An essential but often overlooked component to systemic measurement is direct patient feedback. An antidote to anecdotes, asking patients to spell out their experience in their own words is vital to understanding how the industry is performing. To address gaps in performance, we must include the patient's voice, or improvement plans might miss the boat with respect to future experiences.

Much of Harvey and Jean Picker's work rests on the idea that patients should not only be included in the assessment of care, they should be the *focus* of improvement. The Picker work often cites the negative impact of excluding patients and the downstream effect of having changes made by leaders who fail to include their most important audience: the patients who receive their care. Even with respect to measurement, it can be easy to misinterpret results and drown out the patient's voice in the echo chamber of the C-suite. Therefore, every measurement plan under consideration by leadership must not only include the patient's voice, it must place it front and center.

As documented in earlier chapters, HCAHPS became the direct, mandated intervention to ensure that patient feedback was being put first. However, what was the impact of HCAHPS inside healthcare organizations? The idea of having activity mandated puts a whole new spin on efforts to improve patient experiences. When a large outside entity requires you to do the work you were inspired to do on entering the profession (and perhaps thought you were already doing successfully), the process can be an adjustment.

While working to embrace this mandated form of measurement, healthcare leaders must take a balanced approach. How do you make the mandate your own? How do you ensure that employees are actively engaged in the mission and not just complying? How (and why) do you create your own measurement plan without it feeling reactive? These questions place a great imperative on the shoulders of senior leaders: Tap into your workforce's natural passion and ambition or face a crowd of skeptics.

TOP DOWN

The move to improve the patient experience landed with a large thud in the C-suite of every healthcare organization. As HCAHPS demanded more and more executive attention and became bound to reimbursement, the C-suite and CEOs in particular seemed to move measurement strategies higher up the priority list to increase excitement and employee engagement. To avoid the risk of HCAHPS being perceived as a "check-box" initiative, many executives pushed patient-centered care as a transformative effort worthy of top priority in the strategic planning process (Penso 2017).

How did things go early on? It is unclear if HCAHPS led to much improvement in patient care in its first few years. When the Affordable Care Act (ACA) was enacted in 2010, it stole some limelight from the HCAHPS movement. But HCAHPS and the ACA were intertwined. Many saw HCAHPS as a way to measure and add value to the new experiences of patients under expanded forms of healthcare coverage.

Driven by the ACA and the greater movement to reform healthcare, the shift to value-based purchasing (VBP) occurred in 2012. Born out of frustration with rising costs and middling patient satisfaction, the idea was to move from volume and fee-for-service models that created incentive to overtest and overcharge patients (Porter and Teisberg 2006) toward a model that relied on care demonstrated to be clinically necessary and the ability to keep a population healthy over time in order to receive full reimbursement and even bonuses from the Centers for Medicare & Medicaid Services (2017). At the time, VBP was described as a bold step with the aim of "transforming Medicare from a passive payer of claims to an active purchaser of quality healthcare for its beneficiaries" (Borah et al. 2012). On inception, VBP quickly moved to the forefront of the greater reform movement and transcended HCAHPS as the focus of efforts toward improving the patient experience (Japsen 2015).

Whether you lived through these quick-hitting eras or not, you can feel empathy for healthcare leaders trying to keep up with the latest change. For many, the sole constant was an aspect of the measurement movement in which they were entangled: executive compensation tied to HCAHPS scores. Many healthcare leaders have some form of compensation or bonuses tied to organizational performance on the HCAHPS survey. SullivanCotter's 2019 executive compensation survey shows that 32 percent of total direct compensation is now composed of performance-based incentives, of which about 15 to 20 percent are based on HCAHPS/patient satisfaction, and this percentage has increased over the past ten years. This form of compensation can become a double-edged sword in the minds of executives. If everyone is measuring the patient experience, determining what to fix and moving in lockstep to accomplish it, then a just reward for all these efforts would be a bonus at the end of the year. However, if results aren't great—or at least not good enough to hit the organization's goal—then HCAHPS could become a source of frustration and elicit doubt regarding whether the data are painting a true picture of performance or if the system is rigged.

As Dr. Robert Wachter of the University of California, San Francisco, lamented, "The focus on numbers has gone too far. We're hitting the targets but missing the point" (Wachter 2016). The point, Dr. Wachter argued, is that while measurement is a good idea, it has become a fad that has spun out of control. Physicians and executives alike are chasing their own ratings and losing focus on their patients. Dr. Wachter also argued that computerized systems such as electronic medical records have robbed physicians of true patient interaction, and that hitting numbers has replaced satisfaction derived from providing real human care. "Our businesslike efforts to measure and improve quality are not blocking the altruism, indeed the love, that motivates people to enter the helping professions," he explained. "While we're figuring out how to get better, we need to tread more lightly in assessing the work of the professionals who practice in our most human and sacred fields" (Wachter 2016).

Dr. Wachter is not the only one to have noticed this sweeping problem. Over the past several years, the movement toward measurement has become a culture of overmeasurement, confusion about what to measure, and disdain for survey tools and the leaders who pushed them. A general feeling surfaced that the surveys seem geared toward what patients want out of an experience rather than actual medical outcomes, and that physicians may be engaging in inappropriate medical practices (e.g., prescribing unnecessary drugs to complaining patients) to avoid negative comments on surveys (Zgierska, Rabago, and Miller 2014). This feeling has pushed healthcare leaders to question, if not disagree with, the HCAHPS approach altogether.

One question we have asked is whether one person in an organization can influence the composite HCAHPS score of that organization. To better understand this issue, we need to look at the structure of the typical healthcare organization.

SYSTEMNESS

"Systemness" is another organizational trend that has changed the healthcare landscape. In 2005, The Governance Institute defined systemness as health systems attempting to "look and act more like a single, integrated organization rather than a collection of independently functioning pieces" (Bader et al. 2005). The days of mostly independent hospitals have drawn to a close. As of 2017, 66 percent of hospitals were part of a system that consists of two or more acute-care hospitals (American Hospital Association 2020). Most consumers support the idea of a system, with the majority (65 percent) now preferring to choose a hospital that is part of a system rather than one that is not (NRC Health 2014). Consumers have many reasons for shifting toward the system concept, including the belief that systems can simplify their care journey by tying together the disparate episodes of treatment they will receive. Consumers' chief hope is that systems can deliver coordinated care (NRC

Health 2014), which many believe is sorely lacking. Independent hospitals often struggle to provide comprehensive care and don't always have the resources available to better coordinate care.

Things look different on the inside of a system. Consolidation almost always means layoffs, so when a system is assembled it can be a rough ride for employees. Typically, a system office is established to better oversee the operations of different hospitals and the larger footprint of care sites, as well as to project impartiality among all employees. But the leaders inside these system offices often spend more time with each other than they do at the many care sites under their corporate umbrella. Managing disparate care sites can be difficult; the idea of one-size-fits-all metrics and standardized measurement and reporting processes is the ultimate aim of most systems.

Charging only a handful of people to oversee an entire system's metrics usually results in executives reviewing a dashboard of ten or fewer metrics. We have seen three notable effects of this reduction in metrics. First, most of the HCAHPS survey has become trivial compared with those few metrics that are considered dashboard worthy: willingness to recommend, physician and nurse communication, and overall rating. Second, when those few metrics are not sufficient or the findings are disappointing, leaders tend to continue focusing on them and fail to look at the interconnectedness of the entire survey and the other, ancillary metrics that need to be tracked to drive greater improvement (such as room cleanliness and noise level, comprehension of medication instructions, and postdischarge clarity and confidence). Finally, this maddening focus on such a sliver of the overall survey, coupled with the tie to executive compensation, has caused many to lament the entire movement toward patient-centered care (Johnson 2014; Quick Leonard Kieffer 2016).

This effect of "measurement madness" has increased over the past few years and created an ironic reality: We seem to be unable to focus on measurement at a time when patient expectations and consumer costs have heightened the call for better quantification of our performance (Moore 2019). For example, take a typical hospital that used to measure 5 or 6 concrete metrics such as patient infection rates or average length of stay. Now, it is flooded with 36 patient experience metrics, 22 employee engagement key performance indicators, and 8 organizational culture indicators. From the outside, the organization may seem to be highly committed to quantifying its performance, but from the inside, executives and managers are likely suffering from data disorientation. When too much is being measured, it is difficult, if not impossible, to understand what matters most to patients. The patient voice can easily be drowned out in the cacophony of corporate performance measurement.

Inside the swirling storm of measurement, a question remains: Who hears the patient voice? Who is aware of the HCAHPS metrics within and throughout the organization? Who actually sees the metrics? Typically, a leader in quality "owns" the patient voice and oversees the ins and outs of the survey process. This person or team can report out to other leaders—or not. What if some metrics aren't rosy? What if they are going in the wrong direction and the cause is unknown? Does the quality leader or team want to share these results with the CEO and board now, or are they more likely to wait a month or two and see where the numbers are at that point? Without clear lines of responsibility and a strong push for reporting, it can be easy to gloss over HCAHPS and leave employees in the dark regarding their own performance.

Even when regular reporting is achieved, communicating the findings to employees is a challenge. While CEOs may issue an all-employee memo, and senior leadership may be well briefed on the numbers, middle managers are the key to employees understanding the performance measurements (Munch 2017). Without a dedicated focus on middle management—an often overlooked layer in a complex healthcare organization—it is easy to imagine a nurse or security guard having little understanding of HCAHPS or hearing only a distorted version of what leadership is trying to accomplish. When communication isn't clear or a topic is poorly explained (whether intentional or unintentional), healthcare employees, like most people, will fill in the blanks and form their own conclusions. This game of telephone can create substantially different realities from those intended by senior leadership.

This problem can be exacerbated by systemness. When an organization has grown substantially and includes many locations with differing cultures, it is easy for messages to be stretched and twisted or, worse yet, go undelivered to all who need them. When independent hospitals existed with a single leadership team and board, CEOs could more easily communicate with a smaller number of employees who were part of a single culture.

Despite these challenges, are systems better able to achieve patient-centered care? A comparison of HCAHPS performance in independent hospitals and systems shows that systems perform better, but only slightly (see exhibit 5.2).

NRC Health (2019) has seen slow and steady improvement, the most substantial being 7 points on any given composite HCAHPS score over the past decade. Although this finding may not seem significant, when we consider that it pertains to 4,000 hospitals and about 3 million patients a year, an annual improvement rate of only 1 percent results in 30,000 patients receiving improved care.

Whether it is measurement overload or the challenge of growing systems, these issues are at the heart of healthcare. Are we providing the best possible patient experience? How do we know it's the best? Answering these questions often requires us to explore a subworld within the industry: quality.

A WORD ABOUT QUALITY

Quality is probably the most widely used measure of performance in healthcare today. Measuring quality began before HCAHPS and even predates the original Picker work. Though it originally came about as a tool for physicians to assess medical performance, quality morphed into a larger, more nebulous concept to describe the

EXHIBIT 5.2: Independent Versus System Hospital Performance on HCAHPS

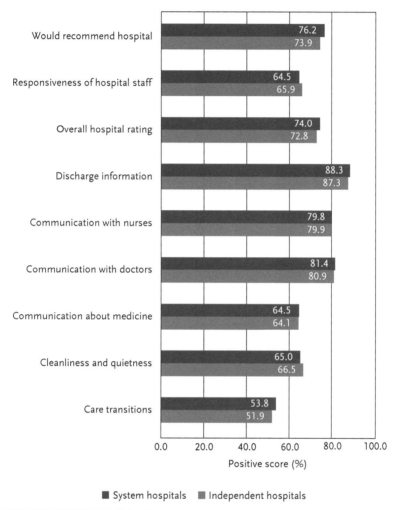

Would recommend hospital: System hospitals 76.2, Independent hospitals 73.9
Responsiveness of hospital staff: System hospitals 64.5, Independent hospitals 65.9
Overall hospital rating: System hospitals 74.0, Independent hospitals 72.8
Discharge information: System hospitals 88.3, Independent hospitals 87.3
Communication with nurses: System hospitals 79.8, Independent hospitals 79.9
Communication with doctors: System hospitals 81.4, Independent hospitals 80.9
Communication about medicine: System hospitals 64.5, Independent hospitals 64.1
Cleanliness and quietness: System hospitals 65.0, Independent hospitals 66.5
Care transitions: System hospitals 53.8, Independent hospitals 51.9

Positive score (%)

■ System hospitals ■ Independent hospitals

Source: NRC Health (2019).

overall performance of the organization, and even strength of the brand as perceived by consumers. Today, many healthcare leaders and healthcare improvement entities lump patient experience and patient safety under the overall quality umbrella.

Conversations about quality often excluded the employees who were tasked with delivering it. Much like HCAHPS felt forced upon physicians, nurses, and other frontline caregivers, the quest for quality became a corporate motto that didn't seem to stick in hospital hallways. Caregivers have often cited their own lack of resources and personal burnout as critical on-the-ground barriers to the larger organizational goals for quality (Vibberts 2018). It matters not what leadership says if managers and their direct reports—those who physically deliver care—do not feel engaged in the call for quality (Munch 2017).

Quality is equally nebulous to consumers. NRC Health (2017) conducted a sprawling study of what quality means to the average healthcare consumer, and the following quotes tell the story:

- "It means I get the care I deserve."
- "Clean, organized, friendly, technology."
- "I get what I pay for."
- "Treat me like a patient, not a paycheck!"
- "I can't define it, but I know it when I see it."

Healthcare's focus on quality doesn't seem to break through to consumers. When asked to assign different attributes to the hospitals near them, consumers emphasized having the best physicians, being the most conveniently located, providing the most personalized care, and so forth. Quality (as a concept on its own) didn't stand out, even though we've banged the drum loudly.

Ask a hundred consumers to define quality and you'll likely get a hundred definitions. Yet there is a deeper meaning that seems to emerge. When consumers are asked, point blank, if quality is important, they respond that it is. In fact, when NRC Health stacked quality against the many other attributes that consumers seem to value, quality won out (see exhibit 5.3).

How can this be? In their own words, consumers could not articulate the importance of quality. However, when listed as one

EXHIBIT 5.3: Healthcare Attributes Consumers Value Most

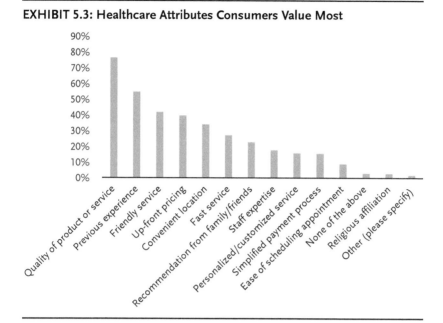

Source: NRC Health (2017).

of many choices in a survey question, quality seemed to be the *most* important attribute to consumers.

The design of the question in exhibit 5.3 may point to a key clue regarding the importance of quality to consumers. Respondents were able to choose multiple metrics, and although quality was chosen more often than any other, most consumers chose at least one (if not two) additional metrics. In fact, the average consumer selected 3.6 factors. Why choose quality when there are other, more understandable metrics? Could it be that quality is seen as a proxy for these other metrics? When you consider the vast array of measures that can be drawn from a company's performance, you might consider the sum of those measures to indicate a high level of quality. When the organization falls flat on multiple factors, lower quality may be perceived. Consequently, everything from convenience to compassion ends up as a proxy for quality. Thus, it is up to healthcare leaders to define quality and demonstrate it to consumers through clear, understandable means. The difference between doing this well and doing it poorly (or not at all) could be the determining factor in whether consumers view a healthcare organization as a success or failure.

THE STRUGGLE TO SUSTAIN RESULTS

Even when success is achieved, sustaining results can be difficult. As much as we have measured and measured over the past few decades, still little is known about how to sustain success. And when an organization reaches the top, there is not much room left to improve.

A change in leadership opens up the risk of a decline in quality and the patient experience (Sfantou et al. 2017; Woods 2016). As much as leaders try to share their approach and build a team effort, the CEO can often be a single point of failure for any given initiative driven by senior management. From a measurement perspective, this possibility highlights the need for CEOs to share metrics widely (i.e., beyond the board and C-suite) to ensure smoother transitions when a leader exits.

Many external factors need to be considered as well. The calls to modernize HCAHPS have grown increasingly louder and are coming directly from hospitals (Bean 2019). This industry turbulence has kept big financial concerns dangling over healthcare leadership. The consistent challenges to the ACA and what may or may not replace it also create a moving target for those pursuing value. Population health efforts also are constantly up against public health trends and a wide swath of aging Americans who are only going to get sicker.

These headwinds must be faced by having engaged leaders, well-communicated visions, and a focus, above all else, on the patient. In the following chapters, we present our updated research on the Picker dimensions and explore what matters most to patients today. We also present case examples and a solution framework for healthcare leaders to consider in order to build and sustain a true consumer-centric culture for the future of healthcare.

REFERENCES

American Hospital Association. 2020. "Fast Facts on U.S. Hospitals, 2020." Updated January. www.aha.org/statistics/fast-facts-us-hospitals.

Bader, B. S., E. A. Kazemek, R. W. Witalis, and C. Lockee. 2005. *Pursuing Systemness: The Evolution of Large Health Systems*. White paper. San Diego, CA: The Governance Institute.

Bean, M. 2019. "Hospital Groups Propose HCAHPS Modernization: 5 Things to Know." *Becker's Hospital Review*. Published July 25. www.beckershospitalreview.com/patient-engagement/hospital-groups-propose-hcahps-modernization-5-things-to-know.html.

Borah, B. J., M. G. Rock, D. L. Wood, D. L. Roellinger, M. G. Johnson, and J. M. Naessens. 2012. "Association Between Value-Based Purchasing Score and Hospital Characteristics." *BMC Health Services Research* 12: 464.

Centers for Medicare & Medicaid Services. 2017. *Hospital Value-Based Purchasing*. Published September. www.cms.gov/Outreach-and-Education/Medicare-Learning-Network-MLN/MLNProducts/Downloads/Hospital-VBPurchasing-Fact-Sheet-ICN907664TextOnly.pdf.

Japsen, B. 2015. "Value-Based Care Will Drive Aetna's Future Goals." *Forbes*. Published May 15. www.forbes.com/sites/brucejapsen/2015/05/15/value-based-care-may-drive-aetna-bid-for-cigna-or-humana/.

Johnson, C. 2014. "The Promises and Pitfalls of Healthcare Quality Performance Measures." Published December 29.

www.chrisjohnsonmd.com/2014/12/29/the-promises-and-pitfalls-of-healthcare-quality-performance-measures/.

Moore, L. G. 2019. "Are We Collapsing Yet? Over-Measurement Is Part of the Hemorrhage in Healthcare Delivery." *3M Inside Angle*. Published August. www.3mhisinsideangle.com/blog-post/are-we-collapsing-yet-over-measurement-is-part-of-the-hemorrhage-in-healthcare-delivery/.

Munch, D. 2017. "Why Middle Managers Are the Key to Quality Improvement Success." Institute for Healthcare Improvement. Published November 22. www.ihi.org/communities/blogs/why-middle-managers-are-the-key-to-qi-success.

NRC Health. 2019. *Hospital Compare Patient Experience Trends*. Lincoln, NE: NRC Health.

———. 2017. *Market Insights Survey of Healthcare Consumers*. Lincoln, NE: NRC Health.

———. 2016. *Patient Experience Survey*. Lincoln, NE: NRC Health.

———. 2014. "Market Insights Survey of Healthcare Consumers." Published in *Seeking Systemness* (white paper). Lincoln, NE: NRC Health.

———. 2008. *Patient Experience Survey*. Lincoln, NE: NRC Health.

Papanicolas, I., J. F. Figueroa, E. J. Orav, and A. K. Jha. 2017. "Patient Hospital Experience Improved Modestly, but No Evidence Medicare Incentives Promoted Meaningful Gains." *Health Affairs* 36 (1): 133–40.

Penso, J. 2017. "A Health Care Paradox: Measuring and Reporting Quality Has Become a Barrier to Improving It." *StatNews*. Published December 13. www.statnews.com/2017/12/13/health-care-quality/.

Porter, M. E., and E. O. Teisberg. 2006. *Redefining Health Care: Creating Value-Based Competition on Results.* Cambridge, MA: Harvard Business School Press.

Quick Leonard Kieffer. 2016. "The Problem with Patient Satisfaction." Published December 11. www.qlksearch.com/blog/problems-with-patient-satisfaction.

Sfantou, D. F., A. Laliotis, A. E. Patelarou, D. Sifaki-Pistolla, M. Matalliotakis, and E. Patelarou. 2017. "Importance of Leadership Style Towards Quality of Care Measures in Healthcare Settings: A Systematic Review." *Healthcare* 5 (4): 73.

SullivanCotter. 2019. *Manager and Executive Compensation in Hospitals and Health Systems Survey.* Accessed February 8, 2020. https://sullivancotter.com/surveys/manager-and-executive-compensation-in-hospitals-and-health-systems/.

Vibberts, M. 2018. "Caring for Frontline Staff Impacts the Bottom Line (with Patient Satisfaction Scores)." Beekley Medical. Published November 16. https://blog.beekley.com/caring-for-frontline-staff-impacts-the-bottom-line-with-patient-satisfaction-scores.

Wachter, R. M. 2016. "How Measurement Fails Doctors and Teachers." *New York Times.* Published January 16. www.nytimes.com/2016/01/17/opinion/sunday/how-measurement-fails-doctors-and-teachers.html.

Woods, C. 2016. "The Role of Leadership in Patient Experience." *Language of Caring Blog.* Published May 11. www.languageofcaring.com/blog-post/role-of-leadership-in-patient-experience/.

Zgierska, A., D. Rabago, and M. Miller. 2014. "Impact of Patient Satisfaction Ratings on Physicians and Clinical Care." *Patient Preference and Adherence* 8: 437–46.

PART II

Dimensions and Stories

CHAPTER 6

Defining a Conceptual Framework: The Dimensions of Patient-Centered Care

THE FOCUS OF this chapter is the Picker Institute's original eight dimensions of patient-centered care, viewed in the context of consumerism. We want to understand the extent to which these eight dimensions are still relevant to today's patients, and how perceptions of the patient experience have changed over time. Lastly, we provide examples of how to apply these dimensions to healthcare in the future.

To review, the eight dimensions of care are as follows (see chapter 1 for the complete definition of each of these dimensions):

1. Respect for patients' values, preferences, and expressed needs
2. Coordination and integration of care
3. Information, communication, and education
4. Physical comfort
5. Emotional support and alleviation of fear and anxiety
6. Involvement of family and friends
7. Continuity and transition
8. Access to care

To assess the continued relevance of these eight dimensions of patient-centered care and the extent to which patients' ratings of their experiences have changed over time, we conducted both qualitative and quantitative research from 2018 through 2019. Both types of research covered the same general topic areas, such as organization of care, communication, courtesy, wait time, trust in hospital staff, emotional support, pain control, the discharge process, and overall impressions about the care received.

STUDY METHODOLOGY

Qualitative Methodology

We conducted qualitative research in three distinct ways. First, focus groups led by a professional moderator were conducted in an online format, with each group composed of eight participants from across the United States. All participants were 18 years or older and had reported a nonmaternity overnight stay at a hospital in the past 12 months. Participants were recruited in collaboration with an organization that maintains a panel of individuals who have opted to share their thoughts and opinions through periodic surveying and focus group participation. Eligible participants received an email invitation to participate in exchange for a small financial incentive.

The second source of qualitative information was a comparison of comments written on patient experience surveys administered during two time periods. The historical perspective was provided by approximately 11,000 open-ended comments on paper surveys administered after inpatient stays between 2001 and 2005. A more recent perspective was provided by approximately 12,500 open-ended comments on paper surveys administered after inpatient stays in 2016 and 2017. We used natural language processing (NLP) to assign themes and sentiments (positive, negative, neutral) to each comment. NLP is a query-based algorithm that uses key word searches to categorize and summarize large quantities of qualitative feedback. The NLP results were then compared between the historical and recent surveys, and similarities and differences were measured.

The third source of qualitative information was open-ended comments included at the end of a quantitative survey conducted in 2019 in preparation for this book (quantitative survey methodology detailed below). Using this format, we were able to assess qualitative feedback from more than 3,000 patients. Various open-ended questions were asked. "If you could do it all over again, what would you change about your actual patient experience?" "Is there anything we haven't asked about? What else is on your mind about your patient experience?" These results were hand coded in order to summarize the findings and identify trends and themes.

Quantitative Methodology

After the focus groups were conducted and the qualitative historical comparisons were completed, we designed a quantitative survey. The quantitative survey was primarily a replication of Cleary and colleagues' 1993 study, which was one of several studies that informed *Through the Patient's Eyes* (Gerteis et al. 1993). In addition to historical questions fielded to replicate the original study, the survey was informed by the results of our qualitative research, and several more survey questions were designed and included.

In their study, Cleary and colleagues (1993) surveyed 3,076 medical and surgical patients from ten participating hospitals. Interviews were conducted via telephone between February and May 1992. Our replication of that study, conducted between July 26 and July 29, 2019, included responses from a total of 3,004 individuals who reported having a nonmaternity overnight stay at a hospital within the prior 12 months. The sample was nationally representative in terms of distribution across the four major geographical regions of the United States.

Similar to recruitment of the focus group participants, respondents to the 2019 quantitative survey were recruited in partnership with a panel provider. Respondents received an email invitation to participate in the online survey in exchange for a small financial incentive.

RESULTS

Qualitative Results

Several common themes arose from the three sources of qualitative information (focus groups, comments written on historical and recent patient experience surveys, and open-ended comments included on the 2019 quantitative survey). Most prominent among the dimensions of patient-centered care were access to care (especially wait time), emotional support, and physical comfort.

Participants in the focus groups confirmed that the needs and desires of patients today are in line with those of patients outlined by Gerteis and colleagues in *Through the Patient's Eyes*. While medical and information technology have advanced since publication of the book, our findings suggest that not much has changed in terms of what is important to patients. According to participants in our focus groups, access to care and emotional support are crucially important to the patient experience and largely determine whether an experience is positive or negative. Although the dialogue included elements of the other dimensions of care, these two concepts were discussed most frequently.

The open-ended comments on the 2019 survey corroborated the focus group findings. When asked about their recent hospital experience, most respondents commented about access to care; information, communication, and education; emotional support; respect for patient preferences; and physical comfort. One interesting finding was a preponderance of patients who indicated that they wished they had advocated more for themselves while in the hospital and undergoing treatment. Respondents indicated that if they had to do it over again, they would "be more assertive," "speak up for myself," and "advocate for myself," and they wouldn't "blindly agree to what [providers] say." These comments speak to the continued importance of the dimensions of respect for patient preferences and information, communication, and education.

Our comparison of comments on historical (between 2001 and 2005) and recent (2016 and 2017) patient experience surveys not only confirmed the continued importance of the eight dimensions of patient-centered care, but also allowed us to understand how the relative importance of the dimensions may have evolved over time. Emotional support and physical comfort were the topics discussed most frequently on the historical and recent surveys. The distribution of comments across the dimensions was remarkably stable in the two study periods. However, as shown in exhibit 6.1, patient feedback categorized as emotional support and respect for patient values increased slightly over time, while feedback categorized as physical comfort and access to care decreased slightly.

Some excerpts from the qualitative feedback include the following:

"I did feel like I had to wait a long time to go to my room and they never explained to me why."

"I felt very trusting of the doctors because of the way they spoke and treated me like they really cared."

"The staff was slow, taking hours to give me the medication needed or said they already gave it to me when they didn't. They were never on the same page of what was going on. The hospital was constantly noisy, so I could never sleep between the pain and the noise. They never even gave me enough medicine to handle my pain and take the edge off. They never offered to help me get out of bed. I couldn't go for walks outside when I was healing and instead had to try to walk in the busy hallways instead of going at my own pace. They didn't explain much of anything."

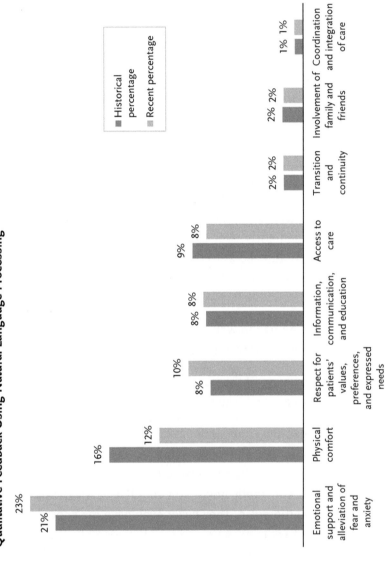

EXHIBIT 6.1: Eight Dimensions of Patient-Centered Care: A Comparison of Historical and Recent Qualitative Feedback Using Natural Language Processing

Source: NRC Health (2019).

"They talked to me while they were taking my information down but ignored me after they left."

"I was given different information from the doctor on duty at night than from the doctor I saw in the day."

"I feel doctors decide on tests and then only reluctantly listen to patients."

"I needed more communication during the stay as I did feel at times very lost about what was going on and what was next."

"I wish family members could stay overnight and until you are released from the hospital."

"I think follow-up is vital and the hospital totally dropped the ball in coordinating my after-surgery care needs."

"I just want to feel like a valued customer."

Looking at the cumulative results of the qualitative research, we find that the eight dimensions of patient-centered care are as relevant and accurate today as they were 25 years ago. All of the dimensions were represented in all forms of patient feedback, indicating that the patient experience is still rooted in and measured by these eight basic needs. Moreover, these qualitative results were confirmed by the quantitative findings.

Quantitative Results

The purpose of the quantitative research was to determine if perceptions of the patient experience have changed since publication of the study by Cleary and colleagues (1993). To accomplish this objective, we compared the results of the 2019 study with those of the 1993 study.

Cleary and colleagues presented their results in the form of "problem scores," meaning that scores represent the percentage of respondents who selected the least optimal (most negative) response option or set of response options. We applied this method to our analysis of the 2019 results to enable comparison. Problem scoring can be useful for quality improvement efforts because it creates a sense of urgency by highlighting areas for improvement. Since publication of Cleary and colleagues' 1993 article, however, the industry has largely moved away from problem scoring in favor of "positive scoring" (the percentage of respondents who selected the most optimal response) because of its alignment with CAHPS initiatives as well as its ease of use.

It is important to note that the information from the 1993 study was gathered via telephone interviews, whereas the 2019 study was fielded via an online survey. Research has shown that survey modes can impact results (Centers for Medicare & Medicaid Services 2008) and that web-based responses tend to be slightly less favorable than those gathered via telephone interviews (Keeter 2015). Additionally, while the original research was conducted with patients who had been recently discharged from one of ten US hospitals, the 2019 study was conducted with panel participants who self-reported a recent hospitalization. Because of these differences in both mode and population, results derived from direct comparisons of scores should be interpreted with caution.

Based on these differences in study methodology, it is not surprising that the 2019 scores tended to be less favorable than the 1993 scores. The average problem score in the 1993 study was 11 percent, while the average problem score across the same items in the 2019 study was 16 percent, indicating that the percentage of patients reporting negative experiences had increased by 5 percentage points on average. If, however, the change in scores over time could be attributed solely to methodological differences, we would expect to see similar changes in each item score (i.e., a change of approximately 5 percentage points for all items). However, the results show that the magnitude of the change over time differs across items and dimensions. These findings suggest that there may be meaningful differences unrelated to methodological effects.

The largest item-level changes (10 percentage points or more) are listed below. Note that all represent more negative experiences over time except for one item in the dimension of Continuity and Transition: "No one on hospital staff told patient when he/she could resume usual activities, such as when to go back to work." Scores for this item improved over time (the problem score decreased from 29 to 18 percent). The items with the largest changes are part of the following dimensions: physical comfort (three items), coordination of care (two items), emotional support and alleviation of fear and anxiety (two items), respect for patient's values, preferences, and needs (one item), transition and continuity (one item), and information and education (one item). Historical and current item scores are listed in exhibit 6.2.

Next, we calculated dimension scores by taking the mean of the item scores within each dimension. At the dimension level, we can see that the largest difference between the current and historical scores is in the physical comfort dimension (problem score increased from 12 to 27 percent, indicating more negative experiences over time), followed by coordination of care, emotional support, and respect for patient values (exhibit 6.3).

EXHIBIT 6.2: A Comparison of Historical and Recent Quantitative Feedback: Dimension Level

Dimension	Item	Historical problem score	Recent problem score	Change over time
Physical comfort	Patient waited more than 15 minutes, on average, after requesting pain medication.	7%	41%	34%
Physical comfort	Patient felt much of his pain could have been eliminated if hospital staff had acted more promptly.	8%	37%	29%

(continued)

(continued from previous page)

Dimension	Item	Historical problem score	Recent problem score	Change over time
Emotional support and alleviation of fear and anxiety	Patient did not get as much help as she would have liked with questions about hospital bill.	2%	31%	29%
Coordination of care	Physician and nurse have conflicting responses to patient's questions.	16%	36%	20%
Physical comfort	Patient waited more than 15 minutes, on average, for help after using call button.	5%	23%	18%
Information, communication, and education	Patient felt physician/ nurse was withholding information.	7%	24%	17%
Respect for patient's values, preferences, and needs	Physicians or nurses sometimes talked in front of patient as if he wasn't there.	9%	25%	16%
Emotional support and alleviation of fear and anxiety	Patient did not get desired help from hospital staff in figuring out how to pay his hospital bill.	19%	33%	14%
Coordination of care	Scheduled tests and procedures usually or always delayed.	4%	14%	10%
Continuity and transition	No one on hospital staff told patient when she could resume usual activities, such as when to go back to work.	29%	18%	−11%

Sources: Cleary et al. (1993); NRC Health (2019).

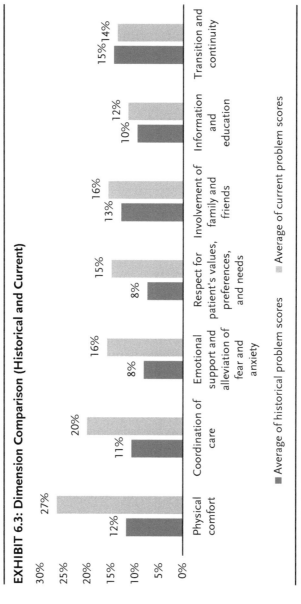

EXHIBIT 6.3: Dimension Comparison (Historical and Current)

Physical comfort: 27%, 12%
Coordination of care: 20%, 11%
Emotional support and alleviation of fear and anxiety: 16%, 8%
Respect for patient's values, preferences, and needs: 15%, 8%
Involvement of family and friends: 16%, 13%
Information and education: 12%, 10%
Transition and continuity: 15%, 14%

■ Average of historical problem scores   ■ Average of current problem scores

Source: NRC Health (2019).

Although we expected to find differences between the historical and current problem scores (with less favorable scores in the 2019 study resulting from methodological factors), some differences exceeded that which we could reasonably attribute to methodology. Those items primarily related to physical comfort, coordination of care, emotional support, and respect for patient values. These results indicate that despite decades of work, improvements in the patient experience are small at best, and, in some cases, patients' care experience seems to be getting worse.

CONCLUSIONS

Evidence from both the qualitative and quantitative studies suggests that the eight dimensions of patient-centered care, developed more than 25 years ago, remain relevant despite the myriad changes that have occurred in healthcare. The qualitative research shows that when given an open forum, patients continue to provide feedback that spans all eight dimensions. However, no evidence of new dimensions was found in the qualitative data. Technology was more often a topic of current feedback than of historical feedback, but rather than manifesting as an additional dimension, it was a common thread throughout all eight dimensions. Many incredible advancements in healthcare-related technology have taken place in recent years: telehealth, the ability to book appointments online, healthcare-related smart phone apps, electronic medical records, robotic medicine. These advancements have created many benefits and led to challenges for patients, and they are tied in their own ways to each dimension. For example, telehealth has led to improvements in access to care as many rural patients are now able to reach their care providers virtually. On the other hand, one challenge in the area of emotional support is the feeling of being ignored as providers type seemingly endless notes into their computers.

Further evidence of the relevance of the eight dimensions can be found in the way in which the patient experience is measured today. Real-time patient feedback often is obtained immediately following a healthcare visit by means of automated Interactive Voice Response calls or online surveys. Few patients are now willing to fill out long-form paper surveys received via regular mail. With this evolution in feedback behavior and newer modes of information collection, the questions asked of patients have needed to change. Fewer, shorter, and more targeted questions are asked to minimize dropouts and maximize responses.

NRC Health partners with hospitals and healthcare systems to collect feedback from their patients using its Real-time Feedback Platform. While healthcare organizations leveraging this solution have ultimate flexibility in the questions they choose to ask patients, NRC Health offers a standard set of questions per care setting, based on decades of research and expertise in the area of patient experience. These recommended questions are rooted in the rich heritage of the eight dimensions but streamlined and modernized for the needs and wants of patients and healthcare organizations in today's consumer-centric world. NRC Health used correlation analyses to discover the topics most important to patients and, in turn, identify the key driver of patient loyalty in each dimension. Simple, targeted question-and-response text was then developed, with simplicity and clarity a top priority. Decades of patient data show the statistical relationship of the eight dimensions with patient loyalty, which is further evidence of their continued relevance.

Healthcare organizations partnering with NRC Health can opt to use the standard set of questions or devise their own questions based on their needs and what they deem to be most important to their patients. In 2019, approximately 84 percent of healthcare organizations opted to use part or all of the standard set of dimension-based questions, suggesting they too believe that these are the most important aspects of the patient experience.

DEFINING THE EIGHT DIMENSIONS OF PATIENT-CENTERED CARE THROUGH THE EYES OF THE CONSUMER

We now understand that the dimensions established 25 years ago remain relevant today. The importance of each dimension has not changed, but how organizations are performing against them has (i.e., patient ratings have largely become more negative over time). When we look at each of the dimensions from a more consumerist perspective, it becomes clear that there are specific things health-care organizations can do to ensure they are meeting the needs of their consumers.

1. Respect for Patients' Values, Preferences, and Expressed Needs

Patients want to be informed regarding their medical conditions and involved in decision-making. They indicate that they want hospital staff to recognize and treat them as *individuals,* as noted earlier. To help meet these needs, healthcare leaders should think of population health from a consumer's perspective— patients are looking at your organization's involvement in their lives long before they enter its four walls. In response, some organizations provide on-site food pharmacies, grocery stores, and cooking classes to remedy food desert conditions in their communities; others offer a gym and wellness programs. Consumers also want to know that they, their families, their values, and their culture will be respected when they are ill. Convey to patients that your organization is committed to helping them, as unique individuals with unique families, values, and cultures, live their fullest lives by getting them back to where they were before their illness (or as close as possible) through improved wellness-focused offerings.

2. Coordination and Integration of Care

People feel vulnerable and powerless in the face of illness, but proper coordination of care can ease these feelings and help patients navigate the often confusing healthcare system. To achieve better coordination, providers need to consider every interaction with consumers and keep in mind that they want to be treated as unique individuals. Organizing support groups for patients who have similar conditions is one way to accomplish this; such groups enable patients to attain a feeling of connectedness. Going one step further and having a physician or nurse lead these groups allows patients to connect with their care providers, which is another deep-seated consumer desire.

3. Information, Communication, and Education

In considering a healthcare system, consumers look for information transparency. Seventy-seven percent begin their healthcare search online, and when consumers search for something online, they are looking for specific information: (1) a convenient way to pay their bill and (2) provider ratings and reviews. Forty-five percent of consumers read online reviews before scheduling an appointment; one out of three say that doing so is their first step in searching for a new provider; and 88 percent trust online reviews as much as a personal recommendation (Donohue 2015). To help consumers find what they are looking for, providers can offer an easy-to-access website with transparent information. When consumers search for online reviews and don't find any, they often feel as though the organization is hiding something, which ties in to patients' often expressed fear that information is being withheld from them or they're not being completely informed about their condition or prognosis.

4. Physical Comfort

As noted earlier, patients' level of physical comfort has a tremendous impact on their care experience. Consumers are looking for a place they know will make them and their families comfortable; they like to see new, clean hospital facilities. Even when a new building is not an option, however, patients' needs for physical comfort can still be met by providing amenities such as additional privacy, more comfortable beds, shower supplies, and access to respite rooms so patients and their families can be made comfortable within the four walls of the organization.

5. Emotional Support and Alleviation of Fear and Anxiety

Consumers with high-deductible health plans are becoming the largest payer in healthcare, second only to the Centers for Medicare & Medicaid Services. Accordingly, they are not only fearful about what could be wrong with them and how physically debilitating it might be, but also about whether it will debilitate them financially. Unsure of the cost of care and whether they will be able to cover it, 23 percent of consumers now delay care altogether, the highest percentage since 2010 (NRC Health 2017). The healthcare future these consumers are demanding involves greater price transparency. They understand that there might be price ranges rather than an exact price, but having a general idea of the cost of care would ease their fears. Barcode scanners, which some hospitals use to keep track of medications and services, also can create stress if there is little or no communication about the scanner's purpose. Providers need to communicate with patients and explain how measures such as these are meant to ensure that the right care is being given to the right patient. Even a heightened focus on the most basic communication about what will happen next and when can have a huge, positive effect on alleviating patients' fear and anxiety during their hospital stay.

6. Involvement of Family and Friends

Consumers involve family and friends from the beginning of their care selection process. As noted earlier, they look for patient ratings and reviews, and these include recommendations from family members and friends. Patients also heal more quickly when family and friends are involved in their treatment, so the more that healthcare organizations can accommodate loved ones, the better the healing environment will be. Providers need to allow family members and friends to spend time with the patient and help them find appropriate ways to advocate for and support their loved one. Those family members and friends designated by the patient as caregivers should be included in clinician-led patient discussions; they also should be kept well informed about the patient's condition and what to expect after discharge.

7. Continuity and Transition

Consumers want to be sure that if they are admitted to a hospital, they will be able to return home as soon as possible. They want to recover completely, and are often nervous that if they go to the hospital, they won't come home or won't know what to do when they go home. Accordingly, the more information made available online (e.g., discharge instructions, follow-up appointments needed), the better. In addition to being educated about various conditions, consumers love to see evidence of the hospital's focus on wellness, such as recipes and organized support groups for individuals with their conditions. When these types of resources are made available to patients, they will be less nervous about their diagnosis or about receiving care.

8. Access to Care

When most healthcare leaders think of access, they think of wait times in their hospital or visitors' ability to park at and navigate the hospital campus. When consumers think of access, they begin with the internet and the hospital's offerings. According to a 2017 NRC Health study, 51 percent of consumers say that convenient and easy access to care, health insurance coverage, and provision of the type of care they are seeking are the most important factors in their decision-making process. They also want a quick visit—hence, the 500 percent increase in retail clinic growth since 2006—and simple online appointment booking (Burkle 2011). Today's consumers don't want to call and wait to speak with someone to book an appointment; they want to go online, read a provider's ratings and patient reviews, and click a button to schedule an appointment. Internal customers, such as physicians within the system, like being able to show the same ratings and reviews to patients when making a referral.

To better understand what is most important to consumers, providers have to ask the right questions at the right time. LaVela and Gallan (2014) found that the mode, timing, and frequency of feedback solicitation can influence survey scores. We found that email was the optimal modality (55 percent of patients preferred this mode, more than five times the percentage who preferred postal mail [10 percent] or telephone calls [11 percent]). Regarding timing, consumers want to provide feedback on a regular basis: 44 percent stated their preference to give feedback after every episode of care. However, consumers want surveys to become available quickly: 83 percent said they would prefer to give feedback within a few days after their visit, 19 percent said they preferred to give feedback within a few minutes, and only 4 percent said they would rather give feedback one week or more after their visit (NRC Health 2017).

The next chapter examines how top-performing healthcare organizations across the country are using the eight dimensions to create a consumer-centric culture.

REFERENCES

Burkle, C. M. 2011. "The Advance of the Retail Health Clinic Market: The Liability Risk Physicians May Potentially Face When Supervising or Collaborating with Other Professionals." *Mayo Clinic Proceedings* 86 (11): 1086–91.

Centers for Medicare & Medicaid Services. 2008. "Mode and Patient-Mix Adjustment of the CAHPS Hospital Survey (HCAHPS)." Published April 30. https://hcahpsonline.org/ globalassets/hcahps/mode-patient-mix-adjustment/final-draft-description-of-hcahps-mode-and-pma-with-bottom-box-modedoc-april-30-2008.pdf.

Cleary, P. D., S. Edgman-Levitan, J. D. Walker, and M. Gerteis. 1993. "Using Patient Reports to Improve Medical Care: A Preliminary Report from 10 Hospitals." *Quality Management in Healthcare* 2 (1): 31–38.

Donohue, R. 2015. *The Consumer Is the New Payer in Healthcare: A Walkthrough of NRC Health's Landmark Study on How Consumer Perceptions Drive Market Realities in Healthcare.* NRC Health white paper. Accessed February 17, 2020. https://nrchealth.com/wp-content/uploads/2017/05/ The-New-Payer-White-Paper_V8.pdf.

Gerteis, M., S. Edgman-Levitan, J. Daley, and T. L. Delbanco (eds.). 1993. *Through the Patient's Eyes: Understanding and Promoting Patient-Centered Care.* San Francisco: Jossey-Bass.

Keeter, S. 2015. "From Telephone to the Web: The Challenge of Mode of Interview Effects in Public Opinion Polls." Pew Research Center. Published May 13. www.pewresearch.org/methods/2015/05/13/from-telephone-to-the-web-the-challenge-of-mode-of-interview-effects-in-public-opinion-polls/.

LaVela, S. L., and A. S. Gallan. 2014. "Evaluation and Measurement of Patient Experience." *Patient Experience Journal* 1 (1): 28–36.

NRC Health. 2019. Unpublished quantitative survey data.

———. 2017. *Market Insights Loyalty Study.* Lincoln, NE: NRC Health.

CHAPTER 7

Best Practices: Case Studies
of Dimensions in Action

THE TERM *consumerism* in healthcare has been starting to gain traction. Most organizations are measuring the patient experience to better understand what they can do to improve that experience within the four walls of the organization. Organizations are also focusing on how to attract more patients or consumers to their facilities. What makes the top organizations in the country unique? Why do consumers choose a particular healthcare organization over others that may be closer to home? How are the top organizations implementing the eight dimensions of patient-centered care to create a better patient and consumer experience? This chapter provides answers to these questions from seven top hospitals and health systems across the country (*U.S. News & World Report* 2019).

The leaders of these organizations share insights on how they are differentiating themselves regarding the consumer experience and how they know they are improving. These leaders understand they have an obligation to be diligent stewards of quality and patient experience, and they ensure that what they ask their staff to do to make improvements aligns with what matters most to their organization and the people involved (consumers, caregivers, staff, and patients). These leaders invest time with their executive teams, organizing their teams' work around what they are trying to accomplish. They then look at key results to demonstrate that they are in fact moving the needle. As these stories illustrate, these organizations are not at the top because of measurement alone; they are at the top in their consumers' eyes because they have provided them with a seat at the table.

UNIVERSITY OF CALIFORNIA, SAN FRANCISCO

Picker Dimensions: Respect for patients' values, preferences, and expressed needs; emotional support and alleviation of fear and anxiety; coordination and integration of care; involvement of family and friends; information, communication, and education

The University of California, San Francisco (UCSF) is driven by the idea that when the best research, the best teaching, and the best patient care converge, breakthroughs can be achieved that help heal the world. Following that principle, UCSF's Helen Diller Family Comprehensive Cancer Center combines basic science, clinical research, epidemiology/cancer control, and patient care from throughout the UCSF system to advance the organization's unique holistic cancer program.

Staff members do everything they can to keep the patient at the center of their focus. All care follows a coordinated, multidisciplinary approach to keep patients from having to go multiple places for appointments with different specialists. That kind of bouncing back and forth between offices is typical of cancer care in general, but not at UCSF. There, many subspecialists within cancer treatment—experts in everything from radiation oncology and medical oncology to nutrition and psychology—come together as a care team to treat each patient, and they make sure that the patient's family and friends are involved as much as possible at every step. Doing so helps the patient feel less anxious and fearful, which creates a better environment for healing.

Anticipating the patient's needs has always been at the forefront of UCSF's approach to cancer care. Knowing that patients with cancer typically need to undergo imaging, for example, the facility's designers built 19 types of imaging modalities to keep patients from having to make stressful trips between testing locations. Pain management experts also are on staff, as well as people known as *symptom-management personnel,* who work side by side with physicians to reduce patient suffering. Understanding that patients come from far away to seek cancer care at UCSF and thus have a variety of logistical and emotional needs, the hospital employs psychologists, support group specialists, and social workers, and offers services such as transportation, parking, and assistance with hotels. These services not only take care of the logistics that can cause anxiety for a patient, but they also help meet the patient's emotional needs. This type of service is what sets UCSF apart when it comes to the patient experience.

Coordination and Integration of Care; Involvement of Family and Friends

What patients love most about UCSF is feeling like the entire team is fighting the cancer on their behalf, anticipating problems or challenges, and preventing them if possible. One example of this commitment involved a patient who had head and neck cancer, a difficult cancer to treat. The patient's options were surgery, radiation, or chemotherapy. The team described the side effects of radiation with this type of cancer, including an inability to eat and/ or excessive salivation or drooling. A nutritionist covered nutritional support with the patient and family members so that everyone understood the next steps, including which foods should be avoided (e.g., hard-to-swallow foods) with this type of cancer and which foods are beneficial (e.g., calorie-dense, high-protein foods). The nutritional specialists at UCSF have expertise in nutrition for patients with cancer. In this example, the team of specialists were dialed in on the patient's type of cancer and knew how to support the patient and family, both medically and emotionally.

Respect for Patients' Values, Preferences, and Expressed Needs

When the UCSF Helen Diller Family Comprehensive Cancer Center's new building, the Baker Precision Cancer Medicine Building, was designed several years ago, patient preferences were taken into account from the beginning. In the earliest stages of design, the center's leaders conducted journey mapping with patients, projecting how the best possible hospital experience would look and feel from their perspective and translating that vision into the center's architecture and patient flow.

The results of this attention to detail are visible. Beautiful artwork is everywhere in the building, from paintings and hanging quilts to quotes on the hallway walls and in the examination rooms. High-quality furnishings are placed throughout the facility, and color palettes are soothing and harmonious. The result is a relaxing environment, which keeps patients from feeling that the surroundings are sterile, cold, or dull. Even chair positioning is taken into account to keep patients—many of whom spend much time in the same chair over repeated visits—from facing a blank wall, which could lead their minds to wander and provoke greater anxiety. (The importance of surroundings is especially true in the infusion room, where chairs for patients command the hospital's best views of the city and bay.)

Spaces in the center were designed with the same patient focus. Recognizing that some patients prefer privacy, while others enjoy the company of other patients when undergoing treatment, UCSF's leaders built large infusion areas to allow for both private rooms and open spaces. Some spaces are furnished with high chairs at counters where patients and family members can plug in laptops; others have swivel chairs arranged in circles around tables to create a comfortable living-room feeling. Large picture windows overlook the water, adding to the space's sense of serenity. In addition, private consultation spaces have been incorporated into the center just off the waiting areas. Staff members can use these spaces to discuss diagnoses and treatment plans in private, and patients can use them to discuss treatments with their providers or have time alone or with family and friends after receiving a difficult diagnosis.

With all this space (and variety of spaces), one might think it would be difficult to locate a patient. However, UCSF uses an electronic location system. Everyone, from staff members to patients, wears an electronic badge that can be located immediately. Monitors allow staff members to view patients, which allows them to sit or stand wherever they feel most comfortable while waiting to be seen.

Just as patients were involved in the design of the new building, feedback was also solicited from internal customers, faculty, and staff members. Adjustable workstations, with desks that can be raised or lowered for sitting or standing users, allow for flexibility. Staff members are given multiple computer monitors to increase their efficiency and comfort; receptionists have the best-quality telephones with headsets that allow them greater freedom of movement; and plenty of desk space is provided in team rooms for physicians and other providers to use. Even on-site laundry services are offered to white coat providers to ensure that they don't have to use their days off for work-related chores.

All of this helps create a better work–life balance for UCSF staff, which is important to the organization's leaders. Recognizing that burnout is on the rise among physicians—especially those who work with patients with cancer—UCSF leaders track their engagement throughout the year, following engagement scores, rewarding high-performing areas, and offering assistance to lower-performing areas. Leaders meet with staff members at hiring, as well as at their 60-day mark, to reinforce the mission-driven culture of the organization. Because staff members have made a conscious decision to follow this particular calling, UCSF's leaders are able to emphasize their personal commitment to the work and keep burnout to a minimum.

Interpersonal skills also are essential in this environment. During the highly emotional experience of cancer treatment, patients and their families often make close connections with staff members and express their gratitude to them afterward. Hospital leaders strive to foster such engagement. When patients respond to surveys and write comments recognizing staff members, UCSF leaders send a letter—including the patient's comment—to the staff members thanking them for their contribution. When a patient dies, UCSF makes time and creates safe spaces for staff members to grieve.

Information, Communication, and Education

One of the best ways UCSF keeps the lines of communication open with patients is through its many Patient Family Advisory Councils (PFACs). There are separate PFACs for Pediatrics and Adult Services, as well as department-focused PFACs, focused solely on the patient experience. The Adult Cancer Service's PFAC is currently run by a former patient who has a master's degree in public health. Once a year, the PFACs come together at a retreat, where patients are invited to speak directly with the CEO, Mark Laret, about things UCSF needs to work on or is doing well. Crucial adjustments to the organization and its processes have come out of these gatherings, including some much needed refinements of the patient portal.

Many organizations outside of healthcare succeed with consumers because they are able to bring them to the table and elicit feedback about what they like and don't like. UCSF has embraced this concept with its PFACs and other measures, and it ensures that a consumer voice is always weighing in on everything the organization does. This emphasis has created a culture of accountability within the organization, as well as a lasting and self-reinforcing consumer-centric culture.

MAYO CLINIC HEALTH SYSTEM

Picker Dimensions: Respect for patients' values, preferences, and expressed needs; coordination and integration of care; access to care

Respect for Patients' Values, Preferences, and Expressed Needs

All 68,000 Mayo Clinic employees work together with the sole purpose of putting the patient's healthcare needs first—no matter where they live. As a values-centered culture, anyone at Mayo Clinic can tell you what its primary value is: *The needs of the patient come first.* The origin of that primary value traces back to more than 150 years ago when Mayo Clinic began as a single-physician medical practice on the Minnesota prairie in 1864. In August 1883, after a devastating tornado tore through Rochester, Dr. William W. Mayo, along with his sons, Will and Charlie, and the Sisters of Saint Francis took care of the injured. Mother Mary Alfred Moes proposed establishing a hospital, with the Mayos serving as staff physicians and the Sisters of Saint Francis providing nursing care.

The uniqueness of the partnership between the Mayos and the Sisters—a partnership of brains and heart—and of the values they espoused set up Mayo Clinic for excellence in two areas: care and service. In 1910, Will Mayo visited Rush Medical Center in Chicago and addressed students in its medical school class, who asked him for Mayo Clinic's secret to success. Mayo told the students, "The best interest of the patient is the only interest to be considered, and in order that the sick may have the benefit of advancing knowledge, union of forces is necessary." Today that translates to "The needs of the patient come first, and we're going to work as a team to take care of that patient and his or her family."

A strong culture rooted in the values of the organization is key to a high-performing health system. How do you build such a culture? It starts with the hiring process—making sure the organization is hiring the right person for the right position. Mayo Clinic's leaders ensure they are hiring the right person by first gaining a better understanding of the candidate's philosophy on teamwork. This is a key to their success; Mayo Clinic focused on team-based care before it became a best practice in the industry. Leaders also make sure that when they consider a candidate, they're not just looking for a person who's a good fit for the organization, but also one for whom the organization is a good fit.

Once hired, the employee goes through the typical orientation and training process that occurs in all health systems, but leaders at Mayo Clinic also make sure to discuss the expectations that come along with its culture, which everyone in the organization lives and breathes. For example, when a physician is paged, he is expected to always answer the page unless he is in an urgent situation with a patient. Before cell phones, the organization had multiple phone stations that were labeled "For Mayo Physician Paging Only." With the ubiquitousness of cell phones, things are easier. Expectations like this allow for strong relationships between physicians and patients, as well as between physicians and their colleagues.

To foster a strong culture, healthcare organizations also need to ensure that the values of everyone in the organization align with those of the organization. You can find out a person's values by asking, "What are your priorities here as part of this organization, and what do you think we could help you with to maximize or optimize those priorities?" This starts a conversation with people because it demonstrates that they are important to you. It doesn't matter if the employee is in maintenance or the head of the department of cardiothoracic surgery. Similarly, showing patients you respect their values, preferences, and needs begins by thoroughly understanding their chief complaint. However, simply walking into a room and asking, "what's wrong?" does not always resonate well or demonstrate the compassion most patients are looking for. This question can be reworded to make the patient feel that he matters and is in the driver's seat: "What are you most concerned about, and what do you hope that we can help you with?" Questions posed this way set a better tone with patients and their families.

Thomas Howell, MD, medical director for patient experience at Mayo Clinic Health System, sees this need for compassion in new physicians, such as his daughter Katy, who is finishing her residency at Nationwide Children's Hospital. She phoned him one day and said she'd been having a tough couple of weeks, but soon realized why. She said, "Just like Winnie the Pooh, I was being a bear of too much brain and not enough heart, so today I decided I was going to be a bear of more heart. I need to remember that when I go in to see a patient and her family, this is their most vulnerable time—it may be the most important interaction they have that day. When I realized that, my day was so much better." By setting the proper tone for yourself and focusing on patients and families, you are being a bear not just of excellent mind, but of excellent heart—and keeping those two things connected is key to a positive patient experience.

Coordination and Integration of Care

Mayo Clinic also provides excellent coordination for patients throughout the system. Mayo leaders and physicians understand that most patients come to them with highly complex problems. When patients walk in the doors at a Mayo Clinic facility, they say they get the sense that it's different and feel renewed hope. Even when patients cannot be cured, they still leave feeling that staff members have truly listened to them, spent time with them, and done everything they could to help. As Dr. Howell mentioned, because Mayo physicians are all salaried, there is a lot more willingness among specialties to help one another. They always think, "What is the best thing for this patient?"

Dr. Howell, the medical director for patient experience, is never concerned about sending a patient to another physician within the health system because he knows the patient is going to be in excellent hands. When there is a change in specialty, all physicians and staff members let the patient know he is going to continue to be well taken care of.

Countless interactions take place in a healthcare system, and not all of them are face-to-face. Yet, if you ask consumers, "How do you decide where to receive healthcare?" their decision is often based on recommendations from family members, friends, and other providers. Despite constraints in access or the predominance of technology in today's healthcare landscape, Mayo Clinic's staff members also recognize that a sense of human touch is needed to build great relationships with customers. Whether the customer is a patient, family member, or staff member, every interaction needs to be conducted in an empathetic way, which involves moving beyond "Midwestern nice" to really trying to understand what the person's priorities are.

When speaking around the world about the work of Mayo Clinic, Dr. Howell is often asked, "What best practices does the Clinic follow to make the organization one of the best in the world?" Dr. Howell responds, "One thing—not one thing only, but *your* one thing as an individual. A person's mission at Mayo is to understand how they can contribute to this great organization that provides great care. If you find your personal *why*, that'll be what makes your day at work incredibly meaningful too, because that's why you're in healthcare in the first place. We never want to get the *what* ahead of the *why*. I think when you focus on that *why*, people become engaged on a whole different level."

Access to Care

Mayo Clinic's leaders understand that people travel from all over the world to their hospitals to receive healthcare. When they think about access, leaders think beyond the four walls of the organization. Recognizing that some patients' needs are complex, that the clinic's locations are not always easy to reach, and that wait times for specialists sometimes can be months—a problem that, given the significant provider shortage in the United States, cannot be solved simply by hiring more physicians—Mayo Clinic leaders have looked for ways to leverage technology to help. Starting with the most in-demand medical specialties, such as rheumatology, they began to triage people using electronic consultations to determine which patients need to come in and which might be served via telehealth. This practice is helping the organization maximize its resources and provide even more value to its patients.

Mayo Clinic also understands that consumers today have choices. Furthermore, the organization considers consumers to be everyone—patients, families, their caregivers, their community—and understands that the best way to compete in a consumerist world is through ease of access. Many people, from patients to students and providers, interact with the clinic in different ways. None of them expect to be asked the same question seven times and be given different forms every step of the way; rather, they expect integration in their experience. One way that Mayo Clinic is achieving this integration is through its experience relationship management (XRM) group, with the goal of becoming an industry leader in XRM.

Through all this, staff members at Mayo Clinic remain focused on the human connection and keep in mind the importance of each interaction. For example, rather than noting that they have performed hundreds of solid-organ transplantations, staff members focus on the hundreds of lives impacted: the patients who are able to go to their daughter's wedding or their son's graduation or do whatever is meaningful to them. They step back and realize that those 500 transplants aren't just a number; they are people, and Mayo Clinic has helped them live their lives to the fullest.

Mayo Clinic's story illustrates how, in today's culture, a healthcare system can embody many of the Picker dimensions. The organization has shown how a strong culture rooted in values can create a better experience for all. Those values have stood the test of time, and Mayo Clinic has consistently remained one of the nation's top healthcare providers for years. Some of its earliest best practices—concepts such as team-based care and salaried physicians—were unique when they were adopted, but many health systems across the country have followed suit. Mayo Clinic's success is difficult to replicate because the organization is grounded in a mindset that keeps the patient at its center and that governs its actions according to an internal *why*. In addition, there is an intangible but enduring commitment among dedicated and caring colleagues. The result is a shared purpose that resonates with patients and the public, and makes Mayo Clinic distinct.

THE JOHNS HOPKINS HOSPITAL

Picker Dimensions: Information and education; involvement of family and friends; continuity and transition; access to care; respect for patient's values, preferences, and expressed needs

Information and Education; Involvement of Family and Friends; Continuity and Transition

The Johns Hopkins Hospital is one of the nation's top hospitals because it is grounded in the mission set forth by one of its first physicians, Dr. William Osler, who said, "It is more important to know what sort of a patient has a disease, than what sort of a disease the patient has." From the beginning, Osler's philosophy of patient-centered care has guided the work of the hospital in its tripartite mission of research, education, and clinical care, serving its patients and the community of Baltimore, Maryland.

Because of its world-class reputation, The Johns Hopkins Hospital serves a diverse population, comprising the residents of Baltimore as well as people seeking care from across the United States and around the world. The Johns Hopkins Hospital not only offers exceptional and leading-edge clinical care, but does so with great compassion.

The providers and staff are passionate about their call to healthcare. This type of workforce creates a culture naturally built around the patient and family experience. The Johns Hopkins Hospital defines the patient and family experience as

> the patient's and family's high expectations of what is about to happen and the *cumulative evaluation* of their journey through our system. Along the way we have opportunities to delight or disappoint based on their clinical and emotional interactions with us, as well as their interactions with our people, our processes, and our physical setting.

This definition guides the continuous improvement approach to patient experience.

Another principle guiding the work is person-centered care, including collaboration, information sharing, participation, and respect and dignity. This is accomplished, in part, through tools of shared decision-making. To this end, The Johns Hopkins Hospital provides patient educational materials, trialed and tested with patients and families. Most patients are assigned educational materials of some type (e.g., videos or printed brochures) to help them better understand their condition. Some of these materials are given to the patient at the bedside, while others are accessed through an assigned patient portal, either at the hospital or at home. The patient portal also includes the patient's vital signs, any medications he is taking, and instructional materials to go along with those medications. Educated patients and families allow for shared decision-making and better outcomes.

Recognizing the importance of involving family and friends in patients' care outside the hospital, especially in cases involving serious diagnoses in which patients' ability to listen can be affected by their illness or emotions, a patient is asked to identify a caregiver whom staff members ensure is present for important conversations. For example, if a patient needs physical therapy after leaving the hospital, therapy staff will make sure that the patient's caregiver is present when they show the patient the required exercises. In this way, the caregiver understands each exercise and can assist the patient, which helps ensure a safe transition home and appropriate follow-through on necessary at-home care.

Another area of focus is the well-being of providers and staff through a wellness program. As an academic medical center, the hospital has physicians who are responsible for the wellness of residents, medical students, and other physicians; it also employs an employee wellness officer and a nursing wellness officer. Support groups are offered for patients with difficult diagnoses as well as for employees and their managers.

Access to Care

As with many hospitals, The Johns Hopkins Hospital has many newer additions and multiple parking lots, and finding one's way can be challenging for patients, visitors, and new staff members. It also can result in increased anxiety and stress. Recognizing this, The Johns Hopkins Hospital staff is always willing to offer help in wayfinding. Part of the organization's strategic plan for the next five years is to "make Johns Hopkins easy" in terms of access. One way it is doing this is by providing a digital wayfinding solution.

In 2020, The Johns Hopkins Hospital will introduce a smartphone app that connects to Bluetooth wayfinding and programs such as Google Maps to allow users to map out walking routes to and from appointment locations in the hospital. The app also helps users locate the nearest cafeteria, ATM, pharmacy, or laboratory, allowing visiting patients and families to find what they need.

Respect for Patients' Values, Preferences, and Expressed Needs

The Johns Hopkins Hospital values the inclusion of patients and families at every level of the organization. Through the use of patient and family advisory councils and volunteer advisers, the voice of the patient and family is included in decisions pertaining to the hiring of executives in the organization and the redesign of buildings and spaces. Patients and families also are involved on key committees. For example, volunteer advisers helped with the selection and implementation of the digital wayfinding app, as well as assisted in designing the hospital's new outpatient cancer center.

Patients at The Johns Hopkins Hospital are also asked to evaluate processes throughout the organization—from the check-in process to online appointment bookings—and advise leadership on how they can be improved. Based on their recommendations, the hospital's leaders have implemented self-scheduling in many clinics and outpatient services. Telemedicine is another program that was implemented in response to patient needs. In the past, patients may have had to face long waits—and the ensuing fear and anxiety—to obtain diagnostic results. The patient portal enables quick access to normal results. However, the patient's provider always calls the patient if the results are abnormal.

To better understand consumer preferences, the hospital also has "patient cafes," focus groups in which people from similar backgrounds (e.g., live in the same neighborhood, have similar diagnoses, or speak the same language) are invited to come in and talk about their experiences at The Johns Hopkins Hospital. Acknowledging that its patients come from all over the country, the hospital also hosts virtual patient and family advisory councils, through which individuals provide remote feedback on a regular basis.

Exhibiting this level of respect for the patient's voice creates a more in-depth conversation at The Johns Hopkins Hospital. This dedication fosters improvement in the patient experience, patient engagement, and patient- and family-centered care, and it encourages staff members to be committed to and consistent in valuing the human connection. Positive patient feedback is not only about great clinical care, but also about feeling comforted and cared about. It is that human connection that The Johns Hopkins Hospital creates, and it is that human connection that successful organizations never lose sight of.

CLEVELAND CLINIC

Picker Dimensions: Respect for patients' values, preferences, and expressed needs; emotional support and alleviation of fear and anxiety; coordination and integration of care; involvement of family and friends; information, communication, and education; access to care

Cleveland Clinic has reframed patient experience as the reduction of suffering and care delivered according to the patient's values. Cleveland Clinic is known around the world for exceptional, safe, high-quality, high-value care. The single variable that makes it unique—the reason patients stay with Cleveland Clinic—is its people. Caregivers, as providers are called, provide groundbreaking medical care because of the technical expertise, innovative spirit, and quality of the organization; however, it's the people who make the experience unforgettable for patients. Cleveland Clinic understands that when consumers seek healthcare, they choose not just with their heads, but with their hearts, and caregivers are deeply committed to the patients they serve and believe in treating everyone like family.

Respect for Patients' Values, Preferences, and Expressed Needs

Cleveland Clinic has a five-year strategic vision built around the personalized patient experience. To that end, the organization wants to know its patients intimately—understand their values, preferences, and needs—and then determine how best to make the organization's message and values resonate with them. Cleveland Clinic started on this path ten years ago when leadership established what has come to be called its "true north," the core concept of "Patients First."

To kick-start the journey toward alignment of patient experience with care delivery, Clinic leaders took 40,000 staff members offline for half a day for an event aptly named the Cleveland Clinic Experience. Institute chairs, neurosurgeons, nurses, medical assistants, environmental service workers, and others came together in a roundtable format to discuss the lifecycle of caregivers and their patients. Participants asked: What does "Patients First" mean with respect to each individual's role here? What are the values of the organization that everyone wants to rally around, and what are the behaviors associated with those values? During the event, leaders rolled out new workplace language to reinforce the concept that everyone at Cleveland Clinic is a caregiver—they exist to serve, and care for, their patients. A homegrown model of service-recovery training was then introduced. Called "Communicate with H.E.A.R.T.," it is grounded in empathy and the recognition that when things (inevitably) go wrong in healthcare, caregivers need to use language that is embodied in HEART: Hear, Empathize, Apologize, Respond, and Thank. For sustainability, the Cleveland Clinic has implemented surveys to gather feedback from patients at the point of service about specific behaviors caregivers should be exhibiting, and these behaviors are built into performance evaluations.

Leadership has since changed, but the organization's alignment with its core concept has never shifted. Caregivers at Cleveland Clinic fulfill patient wishes in every way possible, from hosting multiple weddings and vow-renewal ceremonies to coordinating an on-premises visit of a hospitalized state trooper's beloved horse. Caregivers are relentlessly creative about meeting people where they are, both emotionally and spiritually, and caring for the soul along with the body.

Access to Care

The key to keeping patient experience relevant is hardwiring best practices, as well as innovation. Access is a significant issue for patients. The Clinic implemented same-day appointments years ago as a means of meeting patient expectations. Today, patients can be seen in scheduled virtual visits or 24/7 express care online for urgent issues, and these modes of access are clearly preferred by patients over traditional appointments. The Clinic also adopted Shared Medical Appointments, in which a single clinician sees multiple patients with the same diagnosis at the same time, allowing them to come together and share their experiences. Patients do not want to be defined by their illnesses, and the shared experience of coping with an illness and navigating the journey creates a powerful community. Not only do patients often experience greater satisfaction with shared appointments than with traditional one-on-one appointments, they also have better health outcomes. The reason, of course, is the shared experience: patients together in a room, discussing how they fixed their wheelchairs or how they managed medication side effects. Following tremendous success in this space, Cleveland Clinic is now launching virtual shared medical appointments to create a broader community across the system and expand to less traditional areas, such as bereavement and survivorship programs.

Daily tiered huddles are another new practice. These brief gatherings are held at each level of the organization to discuss issues that matter most to caregivers at that level. The results are reported out to the next level and all the way up to the executive team, which gives everyone in the organization the chance to understand the current state of operations, safety, quality of care, and experience issues, as well as any staffing and caregiver safety needs. Cleveland Clinic has widely adopted Jonathan Bartels' "The Pause," a moment of respect for patients at the time of death and recognition of the privilege to care for them. During the executive-level huddle, leaders pause for a moment of silence after the names of all those who died the day before are read aloud.

Families who have lost a loved one at Cleveland Clinic are also honored in a number of ways. Spiritual care is available for the family within 15 minutes, as is a respectful pause at the bedside to honor the life of the patient, the lives of loved ones, and the caregivers who served the patient. In times of distress, Code Lavenders are also available for patients and their families or caregivers. When called, a team of emergency caregivers arrives to provide moral support and decompression. The Cleveland Clinic knows that there is no exceptional patient experience without caring for the caregivers, who care for patients day in and day out.

To that end, thousands of Cleveland Clinic clinicians have been trained in relationship-centered communication via R.E.D.E. to Communicate, a homegrown model based on evidence of what works in communication tailored to clinical settings. Dr. Adrienne Boissy, chief experience officer, and colleagues conducted a study that looked at 1,500 physicians who completed communication skills training and a matched group of physicians who did not to determine the impact of the R.E.D.E. training on patient satisfaction, provider empathy, and burnout (Boissy et al. 2016). The study findings revealed that no matter the incoming skillset, physician specialty, or years in practice, every physician who underwent training experienced improvement. In addition, a smaller sample demonstrated a significant reduction in burnout, likely because of the community building within the course and empathy modeled to participants. As a result of this study, the R.E.D.E. model has been adopted by the medical school, is embedded in onboarding, and has been expanded to include micro-learnings and complex topics such as opiates, conflict management, and advance care planning.

Designing with the End User: Patients

When patients are partners in their care, they are more likely to engage in care and manage their health. Understanding this, Cleveland Clinic has long had programs focused on listening to patients. In addition to the standard best practices such as bed-side shift reports and purposeful hourly rounding, one of the most powerful practices has been to bring physicians, nurses, and patients together for conversations called "plan of care visits" throughout a patient's stay. Questions during these conversations are of the following nature: What needs to happen to get you home? Are we aligned around when that might happen? These discussions don't sound revolutionary, but organizations often drift from including the patient in the care plan on a daily basis; this is the one intervention that has the potential to increase satisfaction across all domains. These visits also allow for greater transparency regarding the day-to-day care of patients and when they might anticipate going home. In addition, call-back programs and telemedicine are dedicated to patients at high risk of returning to the hospital; paramedics are even sent to some patients' homes to check on them.

Cleveland Clinic hears from patients in a multitude of ways, from the classic focus groups, market research, and patient committees to newer programs such as the Healthcare Partners Program. To become a healthcare partner, a patient can be recommended by caregivers or asked directly by the program; alternatively, they can become involved via a portal on the Clinic's website. Another exciting way Cleveland Clinic has elevated patients' voices is through executive leadership rounds, which include leaders from across the enterprise, as well as board members and healthcare partners. During these rounds, healthcare partners have the opportunity to go out onto the floor with clinic leaders to better understand the current state of the organization and its patients. Consistent board presence on these rounds reinforces commitment at the highest levels of the organization to listening to those they serve, which further humanizes the work of the Clinic and builds a stronger culture of empathy among its leaders. Lastly, during leadership rounds, leaders have the opportunity to do the work of caregivers, which enables them to enrich their understanding of caregivers' lives.

Cleveland Clinic has involved patients and family members as co-creators in their improvements and human-centered design projects. An example is the creation of a single digital doorway for the Clinic. "My Cleveland Clinic" is a unified app experience that houses online scheduling, electronic health record functionality for patient portals, a find-a-doctor tool, and more. During development of the app, patients participated in discussions about its design and functionality. Co-design also impacts clinical care, most recently in the areas of pediatric asthma and access improvement.

With an eye for innovation, consistency, and design, the Cleveland Clinic hopes to always make the mantra "nothing for me without me" a reality for patients around the world.

AKRON CHILDREN'S HOSPITAL

Picker Dimensions: Respect for patients' values, preferences, and expressed needs; involvement of family and friends; access to care; emotional support and alleviation of fear and anxiety

Organizational Culture Sets the Tone for Patient- and Family-Centered Care

Patients and families who visit Akron Children's Hospital consistently say it "feels different" when they walk through the doors of any of more than 60 locations in northeastern Ohio. At the heart of this experience is the hospital's warm and friendly culture. New employees are introduced to the organization's culture during orientation on their first day, and it continues to be emphasized throughout their career. The organization prides itself in demonstrating that working at the hospital is more than a job; it's a calling, and promoting this from within is one of the many ways the hospital maintains its focus on patients and families. This culture also builds staff and leadership loyalty, creating an environment in which they want to stay.

Since its founding in 1890, the hospital has built its culture around three promises:

1. To treat every child as we would our own
2. To treat others as they would like to be treated
3. To turn no child away for any reason

At Akron Children's, every employee plays a role in creating excellent patient and family experiences. Every interaction makes a difference, whether it's a friendly voice when scheduling a visit, walking a lost family to an appointment, or caring for a sick child for an extended period. Patients and families expect high-quality clinical care, but they want that care to be delivered with respect, dignity, and personalization.

Engaging and Collaborating with Patients and Families

Engaging patients and families through social media, the website, and community programs begins before they enter the hospital.

Each facility is designed "through the eyes of a child" and features children's artwork and colorful walls. The atrium lobby at the Akron campus features the "Incrediball Circus 2," an art installation that catches the eyes of young and old alike. Touches like this set the tone for the holistic care that families can expect at Akron Children's.

Another way the hospital engages patients and families is through family-centered rounds. The healthcare team, including attending physicians, residents, and nurses, partner with the patient and family to develop the plan of care, provide bidirectional communication, and clarify medications and orders. The teams strive to contextualize care by asking, "What matters to you?" and getting to know each patient and family. If family members are unable to attend, the hospital provides whiteboards on which patients and family members can write questions for their providers, and the hospital encourages family members to call any time for updates.

Collaboration with family members is sought, not just in the care of individual children, but also for improvement processes, policies, and design projects for new building structures. Akron Children's has one of the oldest parent advisory councils (PAC) in the country; it is a group of patients and family members who use the hospital services frequently and want to give back to the organization. Feedback from these trained volunteers is vital to delivering value-added experience. Parent advisory council members sit on hospital committees, review hospital policies, and advocate for safety and quality. Parent advisers are also members of an interprofessional patient/family education committee, which ensures that evidence-based patient education teaching tools and materials are reviewed for health literacy (including clear and plain language), content accuracy, and cultural sensitivity. For patients or family members who want to be involved and provide feedback but find it difficult to do so in person, the hospital hosts an online parent panel with multiple opportunities to share insights.

Feedback from parent advisers and patient- and family-experience surveys and social media is used by the hospital to recognize physicians, nurses, and other staff members. These team members are recognized with the Chief Moment Officer award, which is given to staff members who have left an impression on a family that resonates with the organization's mission, vision, and values. The award is presented monthly at the hospital's leadership meeting.

Access to Care

Access to healthcare is a priority for Akron Children's, so hospital leaders developed a strategy to build regional health centers with primary care and specialty services. Patients and their families do not have to travel far from their homes to receive care. In addition, the hospital has a growing population health program offering case management, interpretive services, and the assistance of community health workers to at-risk families.

Akron Children's Hospital provides health services in almost every school district within an hour of the organization (68 schools in total). In 2019, it began offering telehealth clinic appointments between school-based clinics and a nurse practitioner located at the hospital or in the clinic. Quickly identifying and addressing the healthcare needs of students decreases their time away from the classroom and enables their loved ones to miss less work. The result is better access and enhanced coordination with the hospital.

The hospital also created new healthcare models that provide convenient ways for patients and families with minor health issues to receive care. One such model, Quick Care, allows families who are unable to schedule an appointment with the child's pediatrician to be seen quickly during the day and early evening.

Lastly, the hospital has expanded access to care through telehealth. Its telepsych program enables patients to go to their primary care office, which may be closer to home than the hospital, for a remote appointment with a psychologist. Having done this successfully for many years, Akron Children's is now expanding this service and looking into other telehealth options for the community's low-acute needs, giving consumers more opportunities to choose the location and medium in which they receive care.

Alleviating the Stress of Healthcare

Staff members at Akron Children's Hospital ensure that patients and families are at the center of all they do. Recognizing that comfort and safety lead to healing, they look at the experience holistically and try to make it as pleasant and stress free as possible. Child life specialists, who are trained in distraction techniques, comfort positioning, and child-specific approaches, are key members of the healthcare team. These specialists reduce patients' fear and anxiety while providing age-specific education and play. They also shape expectations by walking patients through upcoming procedures and allowing patients and family members to look at, and play with, the equipment that will be used.

The hospital offers multiple options for positive distraction, including pet, art, and music therapy. The Doggie Brigade sends animals to visit patients. Occasionally, a visiting pony named Willie Nelson is seen at the bedside. The Emily Cooper Welty Expressive Therapy Center hosts a variety of therapeutic activities and features a recording studio and dance classes for children of all abilities. The Volunteer Services department offers a wide variety of themed activity carts—featuring everything from superheroes to cookies—to help keep children entertained at the bedside.

The hospital also has respite rooms available for families. Both the Reinberger Center at the hospital and the nearby Ronald McDonald House offer services for visitors, including private sleep rooms, showers, consultation rooms, and large kitchens. Because many patients are in the hospital for extended periods, a volunteer-driven hair salon recently began providing services to family members. Various relaxation groups, massages, and mindfulness classes are also offered at respite areas to keep family members relaxed and comfortable.

Family Support

Additional types of support are available to patients and families at Akron Children's Hospital. The Family Resource Center, for example, is staffed by a medical librarian who offers individualized education and specialized kits for families to borrow. To augment the written information, numerous classes such as family CPR and asthma education are offered with hands-on demonstration in a small group setting.

A Parent Mentor Program, which allows peer-to-peer mentoring for families, pairs trained parent volunteers with those seeking an individual who has gone through a similar diagnosis or experience. Using an online database, a family can search by diagnosis or department, read profiles, and contact mentors they feel might be a good fit for them.

The PAC's coffee cart provides another opportunity for families to connect. This grant-funded cart offers coffee and snacks to families on inpatient floors, while providing additional information about the parent mentor and adviser programs. Through encounters such as these, parent advisers can comfort other parents who are feeling overwhelmed by their situation. Doing so creates a community in which patients and families can share their feelings.

Finally, parent navigators located within certain specialties meet with parents of children who recently received a diagnosis to help them navigate the system and find needed resources. Many of the specialists also have personal experiences they can draw upon to provide support to patients and families.

MOUNT SINAI HEALTH SYSTEM

Picker Dimensions: Coordination and integration of care; emotional support and alleviation of fear and anxiety; involvement of family and friends; continuity and transition

Putting the Focus on Patient-Centered Care

Patients come from all over the world to seek care at Mount Sinai Health System (Mount Sinai) in New York City, drawn by the hospital's top-notch physicians and its holistic and innovative approach to medicine.

Patients make Mount Sinai their ongoing healthcare provider, not just because of the quality of its physicians, but also because of the experiences they have with the entire team of people on staff. The Mount Sinai team shares an empathic, engaged culture built around staff members—both clinical and nonclinical—who are committed to their work. This commitment is evidenced in both the quality of care they provide and in their passion for providing an excellent experience to patients and their families. Patients and families who come to Mount Sinai for medical care have described a sense of comfort and familiarity with the staff members who interact with them. They feel well cared for on a personal level, which is a big factor in gaining patient loyalty.

When Mount Sinai became a health system in September 2013, the leadership team understood that to create a cohesive organization from separate hospitals, they would need to promote a cultural transformation that maintained the unique culture and established community ties of each of the hospitals while unifying them as a health system under one set of values.

Initially, Mount Sinai made strong gains in its safety and quality outcomes, but it needed to build upon the good work already accomplished to include the overall experience of care. The transformation and focus on experience of care required a shift from physician-centered care, which had long been the orientation of the organization's constituent hospitals, toward a more patient-centered culture.

The leadership team began by partnering with leading experts from outside the organization to understand how similar health systems achieved a patient-centered approach. Recognizing that staff engagement is a significant component of this cultural work, the leadership administered a survey to all staff members to assess their readiness for a cultural transformation. The survey focused on what patient experience means to each staff member and their role, department, hospital, or medical practice. More than 18,000 employees (40 percent) responded, and the results showed that, overall, the staff was ready to embark on this cultural transformation and understood the importance of placing the patient at the center of its work.

Health system leaders also took several steps to communicate with their employees the importance of removing barriers to care and placing patients at the center of everything they do. They held a series of coordinated town halls at the various hospital sites to share survey results and explain next steps. In the months that followed, groups of key individuals—both patient facing and non–patient facing—at all levels of the institution were invited to participate in several sessions to discuss the organization's values and vision. They also worked with a graphic designer to create what would become a visual guide, a colorful and detailed depiction of what the ideal patient experience would look like at Mount Sinai. This visual guide has now become the centerpiece of a four-hour interactive session, the *Mount Sinai Health System Experience*, which brings housekeepers and physicians together to learn what it means to put patients first at Mount Sinai. All 42,000-plus Mount Sinai employees are participating in this session, which helps the organization educate its employees about the mission, vision, and values of the organization.

A renewed focus on engagement and recognition has been another result of the cultural transformation efforts. Several employee recognition programs have been initiated at the various hospitals and ambulatory centers. One of note is called STAR (Strive to Achieve Relationships), which is currently active at two of the hospitals. It promotes teamwork across departments by allowing staff members to log into a web-based application to nominate any employee for a STAR based on the way the employee exhibited any one or more of the Mount Sinai values: safety, agility, creativity, empathy, and teamwork.

In addition, staff members from various sites came up with a rallying cry, "Better Together," which reflects the organization's emphasis on partnership and community and celebrates the kind of team spirit Mount Sinai stands for.

Coordination and Integration of Care; Emotional Support and Alleviation of Fear and Anxiety

Mount Sinai's leadership reflects true dedication to the exemplary care the organization provides for its patients, as well as the staff's ability to go beyond simply treating a disease to making patients feel truly *cared for* on a personal level. To do this, the organization focuses on key behaviors that drive the overall patient experience, including responsiveness, compassionate and clear communication, welcoming, and wayfinding. The organization ensures that staff members spend more time in front of their patients than in front of a computer by using initiatives such as purposeful hourly rounding, which makes patients feel safe and well cared for throughout the day, and leadership rounding, which entails checking in regularly with staff members to learn if there is anything they need to provide patients with the best experience possible.

Teamwork, reflected in everything from the organization's rallying cry to leaders' responsibility for teaching and role modeling, is the organization's most important tactic in striving for safe, high-quality care. Patients' letters of appreciation often speak to the teamwork they observed among staff members, as well as to the exceptional communication that team members had with each other and with them. This kind of teamwork makes patients feel confident they are in the right place. However, teamwork doesn't happen by chance—there are natural relationship builders and connectors that must be drawn upon. Certain technological advancements, such as electronic medical records, have improved the dissemination of information across platforms and institutions. But even such advancements can create a barrier in healthcare by making it easier for people to avoid face-to-face communication. Consequently, a more patient-focused cultural transformation, such as the one happening at Mount Sinai, is imperative.

Mount Sinai employees have reported that they feel like they are part of a family; realizing that this type of emotional connection helps patients with their healing process, they try to convey this sense of family to them as well. Everyone in the organization does this in different ways, but every job at Mount Sinai—whether it's transporting a patient to radiology or performing heart surgery—comes down to ensuring that patients consistently receive the best care while feeling cared for. The strong connection that employees have to Mount Sinai and to each other enables them to deliver on this promise.

Continuity and Transition

When it comes to care transitions, Mount Sinai focuses on the needs of each patient and their family. Early on, the clinical team works to identify a caregiver for each patient. This individual is included in all important discussions during care and is also engaged with staff to ensure that he understands everything the patient needs to know once back at home. In addition, Mount Sinai is working to make family meetings more commonplace throughout the duration of each patient's care. To that end, the organization has been training staff members to better narrate the care they are providing, so that all questions or concerns are addressed. The staff understands that all patients need clear and simple instructions and messaging pertaining to their illness and the type of care required once they return home. Thus, the staff tries to remain focused on the patient's perspective, rather than being task oriented, and to communicate as often and clearly as possible.

Voice of the Patient

A key component of Mount Sinai's journey toward patient-centered care has been using patient feedback to inform best practices and behaviors. The organization is working toward including patients and family members as partners in every aspect of care in an effort to improve safety, quality, and the overall patient and family experience. Mount Sinai takes a multifaceted approach to incorporating the patient's voice into this work, which includes tracking and trending patient comments on surveys as well as patient complaints and compliments. In addition, the organization recently implemented a Patient and Family Partnership Program to support and expand upon some of the work underway involving recruitment and training of patients and family members to serve as partners with staff at the hospital and medical practice level in efforts such as workflow redesign, patient education, and continuous improvement initiatives. Staff members who work with patient and family partners report that they are more meaningfully engaged in their work and feel that they have a greater impact in the helping and healing process. This work exemplifies the sentiment of "Better Together."

JEFFERSON HEALTH

Picker Dimensions: Coordination and integration of care; continuity and transition; access to care; involvement of family and friends; information, communication, and education

In 2013, Jefferson Health started a new chapter in its storied history. Founded in Philadelphia by the grandson of a Revolutionary War general, Jefferson initially became known for Dr. George McClellan's great innovative idea in 1824: Medical students should participate in the care of patients during their school years, not wait until after medical school, as was the practice.

By 2013, Jefferson was known for its medical school, a historic nursing school, and other health profession schools. It worked closely with the top-ranked Thomas Jefferson University Hospital in a multicorporation governance arrangement. However, that year, the trustees of both institutions decided to combine the university and hospital, and they hired the first modern-day combined president and CEO, Dr. Stephen Klasko, as a change agent to move the historic institutions into the future.

At the time, Jefferson consisted of two hospitals in downtown Philadelphia, an attached third hospital for neurosciences, three boards, six colleges, 12,000 employees, and approximately $1.5 billion in revenues. The separation of the university and hospitals even extended to the email and payroll systems.

Although each of these institutions scored well in national rankings, the trustees believed they were ill prepared for future change in both healthcare and higher education. As president and CEO, Dr. Klasko moved quickly to combine the governing boards and outline a plan for values-driven change that would prepare Jefferson to be a consumer-facing institution (The Governance Institute 2017; Voosen 2016).

Dr. Klasko proposed to the board that Jefferson commit to pursuing two key strategies:

1. **Differentiation:** Jefferson would differentiate itself from the other six academic medical centers in Philadelphia by elevating innovation essentially to the level of a mission and adopting the following values: Put People First, Be Bold and Think Differently, and Do the Right Thing. The vision statement is now: Reimagining health, education and discovery to create unparalleled value.

2. **Proactive jump to the future:** Jefferson would understand what will be obvious a decade from now and commit to doing it today. The core of that transformation would be seeing patients and students as human beings seeking health and education where *they* are.

Both higher education and healthcare delivery face four problems that Jefferson set out to tackle:

1. They both cost too much, with sunk costs in legacy facilities.

2. Patients need to be able to "own" their own medical records (as they do their financial records), and students need to be able to easily track their progress academically using some of the same tools that they now use to track their fitness.

3. Both the traditional academic and healthcare ecosystems have difficulty with transparency and explaining to students and patients how costs correlate with outcomes.

4. Both are ill prepared for a digital future: The "Fourth Industrial Revolution" will change the future of work, while offering revolutionary opportunities to solve issues such as health disparities and access to care.

Jefferson's new vision of reimagining health and higher education essentially meant getting a "195-year-old academic medical center to act like a start-up company." In healthcare, that meant transitioning from a business-to-business model, in which providers sell themselves to physicians and insurers, to a business-to-consumer model in which providers sell themselves to consumers. Just as importantly, Jefferson recognized that people do not view themselves as patients until they are ill. Through its DICE (digital innovation and consumer engagement) group, Jefferson hoped to attract people into its digital web who want to thrive without having health concerns get in the way. Through that model, they will already be part of the "Jefferson health club," making Jefferson easier to access when they need a service.

Concomitant with the new vision was an expansion in the "pillars" that define Jefferson. The old model focused on two pillars (academic and clinical), while the new model added two more pillars: philanthropy and innovation/strategic ventures. In particular, the organization's goal was to harness innovation to master skills needed in the future: bending the cost curve, creating equitable access, redefining the patient experience, and turning population health from a philosophy into everyday practice. Finally, the strategy entailed moving ahead of the market from volume to value (even while getting paid for volume in some cases). To that end, Jefferson embarked on four distinct strategies to differentiate itself from the competition.

Strategy 1. Healthcare with No Address

Just as they shop and bank from the comfort of their homes, consumers want to obtain their healthcare digitally, with no fixed address. To accomplish this, Jefferson Health has launched a variety of programs to better address care coordination and integration, as well as access to care and involvement of family and friends:

- **Virtual visits:** Telehealth will soon become like "telebanking." Although no one uses the term *telebanking*, everyone understands that most banking is done online, except for specific tasks that require a visit to a branch. Healthcare will be much the same—done online, with fewer tasks that require the consumer to find a building. Jefferson organized its telehealth activities by launching JeffConnect, which provides easy and convenient access to a physician through virtual appointments. This program quickly led to an 18 percent increase in new patient referrals, with the largest gains occurring among younger patients. To get physicians on board, Jefferson changed the way it compensates clinicians, offering incentives for those who embrace telehealth. As a result, Jefferson Health boasts perhaps the largest telehealth practice driven by its own faculty across all specialties. In 2019, Jefferson celebrated its one hundredth audiovisual patient visit.

- **Tele-triage:** Almost all nonambulance patient visitors to the emergency department (ED) at Thomas Jefferson University Hospital now speak to a physician immediately via telehealth. The system was critical to handling the 80 percent increase in ED visits in the summer of 2019, when a nearby safety-net hospital in Philadelphia went bankrupt, and Jefferson took on a substantial portion of the diverted emergency load. In its self-insured employee population (35,000 patients and their families), a variable deductible program has been established ($500 if you come to the ED and a $0 deductible if JeffConnect sends you to the ED), resulting in an almost 50 percent reduction in ED visits through telehealth, urgent care, and next-day appointments; $5 million in savings; and increased employee satisfaction and productivity.

- **Virtual inpatient rounds:** Jefferson began a pilot with a video conferencing company to allow family members to participate virtually in inpatient rounds and discharge planning. The same service is used to update family members on their loved one's well-being immediately after surgery.

- **Preventive/screening appointment reminders:** Jefferson automatically sends reminders to a patient's smartphone or smartwatch when it is time to schedule an appointment, such as for a colonoscopy or mammography. Such reminders greatly increase the likelihood that the patient makes the appointment and ultimately receives the needed service.

As part of this effort, Jefferson has changed the way it markets to consumers to improve information, communication, and education. Traditional approaches, such as television and billboard advertising, have been abandoned because they no longer connect with patients. The new approach segments consumers and then targets identified cohorts in different ways. For example, a 65-year-old with a smartwatch and a sleep tracker will respond to online tracking through JeffConnect, while a patient with cancer who is not digitally savvy has a phone ambassador. The goal is to give consumers the information they need to make good decisions about their health, and then help them connect with the healthcare community. Once they connect, Jefferson seeks to inspire long-term loyalty by providing true value for the money, including a single point of contact and a seamless experience across the continuum.

Jefferson Health is preparing for even more dramatic transformations in the provision of virtual care over the next ten years, driven by deep learning, machine cognition, and artificial intelligence. In 2019, Jefferson, through a partnership with a genetic testing company, offered all employees free full genomic testing, and it expects that most hospitals with more than $1 billion in revenues will provide real-time genomic-based decision support at the time a prescription is written. As the decades progress, Dr. Klasko believes a growing proportion of the population with chronic conditions will rely on virtual health assistants to promote wellness and ongoing care management. By 2030, a majority of healthcare interactions will be virtual or at home, and the majority of these interactions will involve artificial intelligence or machine cognition applications.

Strategy 2. Scale Through the Hub-and-Hub Model

Unlike other academic medical centers, Jefferson is not pursuing a hub-and-spoke model where the goal is to funnel patients from outlying communities to a tertiary/quaternary hub in the city. Rather, Jefferson is using a hub-and-hub model with the goal of providing patients access to care in their local communities. To that end, Jefferson completed five mergers and acquisitions with community hospitals in the past four years, allowing merged entities to participate in governance through board seats at an equivalent number to that for legacy Jefferson board members. This unique "governance as currency" model promotes a board that adopts a community mindset and single-board mentality.

Jefferson is a much different place from what it was just six years ago. As of 2020, it has 14 hospitals with 35,000 employees, with planned mergers that would increase the total to 19, along with more than 40 outpatient and urgent care locations that handle 3.8 million visits annually.

Strategy 3. Culture Change

Building a consumer platform in a traditional academic medical center can be an arduous process because academic leaders have been trained in an autonomous and a hierarchical atmosphere. Overcoming these biases requires engagement through every "moment of truth." To accomplish the four-pillar model, with innovation and creativity emphasized as much as traditional academic and clinical skillsets, Jefferson launched an institute, and several leadership development programs played a critical role in spearheading cultural change throughout the organization.

- **Jefferson's Onboarding and Leadership Transformation (JOLT) Institute:** Each year, 40 emerging leaders complete the nine-month JOLT program, which integrates classroom instruction, a project/sketch assignment, and executive coaching. Selected candidates go through an application process and must be sponsored and receive executive approval to participate. JOLT graduates have experienced a 325 percent improvement in their ability to handle difficult issues and scenarios.

- **Jefferson Leadership Institute:** This initiative "reprograms" physicians by focusing on competency development and improving readiness for leadership roles through specially designed projects that include participant and sponsor feedback. The goal is to change longstanding belief systems, overcome perceived limitations and selection/education biases, reduce resistance to change, and avoid burnout. Fifty-four percent of physicians reported at least one symptom of burnout (Shanafelt 2015), and most burned-out physicians remain disengaged from the organization. By contrast, capable and engaged physicians tend to be more productive and feel they can make a difference.

Strategy 4. Going "All-In" on Innovation

At a February 2017 retreat, Dr. Klasko gave Jefferson leaders a choice with regard to pursuing innovation. The first option was to pursue incremental improvement in the clinical and academic pillars, supported by philanthropy, and to pursue innovation and partnerships as a secondary concern. The second option was to make innovation and strategic partnerships the core and driver of the health system's strategic vision and its main differentiator from the competition. Jefferson's leaders chose this second approach, and the management team that oversees the clinical and academic enterprises has been charged with making this vision a reality.

To date, Jefferson has embarked on many strategic partnerships. In aggregate, they account for 25 to 30 percent of Jefferson's entire profits, making them critical to the financial health and vitality of the organization. These profits stem from Jefferson's insistence on taking equity stakes in new projects, not just serving as a pilot site for others. Beyond the financial benefits, Jefferson's leaders ensure that these innovations improve clinical or academic performance such as bending the cost curve, improving revenue cycle performance, and redefining the patient experience. At the same time, beyond the reputational and revenue aspects of these partnerships, they have allowed physicians and nurses to develop critical skills, such as creating equitable access and improving social determinants, and turn population health from a philosophy to everyday practice (rather than innovating for the sake of innovation itself). Examples of these innovative partnerships include the following:

- **JeffDesign:** Jefferson is the first medical school to integrate design thinking into its curriculum. Medical students are accepted into the program without taking the Medical College Admission Test, and they participate in a comprehensive design thinking cohort that explores upstream solutions to acute problems and develops products for market. In addition, to build the medical toolbox, the students join CoLab PHL (Philadelphia), a redesigned Airstream trailer that goes into neighborhoods to engage communities in a design thinking exercise to improve conditions that contribute to the social determinants of health.
- **DICE:** Jefferson Health created its own in-house data and applications team, designed to create forward-thinking solutions for issues facing education and healthcare delivery.
- **Livongo:** This consumer digital health company focuses on the treatment of chronic diseases. The technology-driven continual interaction with patients has shown strong initial results for type 2 diabetes care, including a 28 percent reduction in ED visits and a 39 percent reduction in inpatient admissions.
- **Digitally powered transportation services:** Through this joint venture, Jefferson extends its "healthcare with no address" philosophy by bringing JeffConnect and other

patient services directly into patients' homes, while using "AI-directed" transportation services when patients need care in the office or hospital.

- **Human-centered medical education:** Jefferson is home to the decades-long research that resulted in the Jefferson Scale of Empathy, a validated 20-item scale that focuses on the cognitive skills of empathy and the power it has to improve patient care and experience and allay burnout in clinicians. The goal is to teach health professionals to be ready for what awaits them in ten years, when machines can remember data, but clinicians must be the humans in the room, even if that room is virtual.

- **Nurse safety:** Jefferson recognized an increasing problem related to behavioral health and patients who were perceived as threatening to nurses and other health professionals. Jefferson co-owns and partnered with a digital/GPS company to develop Strongline, which enables a nurse to signal concern for her safety by pressing a small button that silently alerts anyone within the area to come to her aid.

REFERENCES

Boissy, A., A. K. Windover, D. Bokar, M. Karafa, K. Neuendorf, R. M. Frankel, J. Merlino, and M. B. Rothenberg. 2016. "Communication Skills Training for Physicians Improves Patient Satisfaction." *Journal of General Internal Medicine*. Published February 26. https://link.springer.com/article/ 10.1007/s11606-016-3597-2.

Governance Institute. 2017. *One Jefferson: Accelerating Reinvention of Academic Medicine Through Growth, Integration, and Innovation*. Accessed February 28, 2020. www.governanceinstitute. com/page/TGICaseStudies.

Shanafelt, T. D., O. Hasan, L. N. Dyrbye, C. Sinsky, D. Satele, J. Sloan, and C. P. West. 2015. "Changes in Burnout and Satisfaction with Work–Life Balance in Physicians and the General US Working Population Between 2011 and 2014." *Mayo Clinic Proceedings* 90 (12): 1600–13.

U.S. News & World Report. 2019. *Best Hospitals 2019 Guidebook.* Accessed March 5, 2020. https://health.usnews.com/best-hospitals.

Voosen, P. 2016. "Is It Time for Universities to Get Out of the Hospital Business?" *Chronicle of Higher Education.* Published May 16. www.chronicle.com/article/Is-It-Time-for-Universities-to/236643vv.

PART III

Building a Consumer-Centric System

CHAPTER 8

Consumer-Centric Leadership

WHEN THE PROVERBIAL alien visits from intergalactic space, healthcare delivery in the United States will truly be a mind-boggling conundrum. Some features of this conundrum are well known: an immensely wealthy country where health outcomes for its population fall behind those of less wealthy countries. A country where longevity is falling for the first time—many children will live shorter lives than their parents.

But there is a deeper conundrum in healthcare delivery. It is the contrast between the passion, knowledge, and dedication of the American healthcare workforce and the confusing, fragmented, tedious, and inequitable delivery of care to patients. As the examples in chapter 7 demonstrate, healthcare organizations that emphasize the Picker dimensions, every day for every patient, can transform the consumer experience. But many organizations have not yet found the courage to forge ahead on this urgent path.

The consumer revolution in healthcare is nothing less than people understanding that the system itself is sick, and that moving from a focus on "sick care" to "health assurance" will be necessary for the traditional healthcare ecosystem in much the same way as convenience and cost pressures transformed the retail industry.

This revolution includes the use of technology to make everything that is difficult today easier. Think about the banking industry. Not too long ago, banks were the center of the financial world for most consumers, with inflexible hours and transactions that took a good deal of time. Now, approximately 90 percent of banking occurs at home. The same convenience is being demanded of healthcare. As a result, organizations will be rewarded if they can effectively and appropriately use technology to help individuals and their families thrive, while those organizations that remain focused on sick care will go the way of retail organizations that ignored the Amazon revolution. These changes require us to revise our understanding of healthcare so that people are supported at all times, where they are, when they need it, including at home. The revolution places the human at the center of the healthcare journey.

This revolution also includes the fight for health consumer citizenship: the right to understand the costs and outcomes of a treatment plan, the right to own one's own medical records, and the right to access care itself.

Finally, the revolution will be fought by both outsiders and insiders. On the outside, the healthcare delivery industry, dominated by legacy institutions, faces competition from retail medicine, telehealth, the shift to outpatient care for numerous procedures that used to require a hospital bed, and the so-called millennial skimming companies that offer instant digital access to services that once required patients to sit, sometimes for long periods, in the waiting rooms of physicians' offices.

The insider revolutionaries are ready too. Today's medical students are increasingly diverse and deeply committed to social justice. They are keenly aware that social and lifestyle factors account for much more of the long-term outcomes for their patients compared with what they as new physicians can offer in episodic sick care.

In educational circles, the crisis of complex care is front and center. Educators are aware that they are preparing students in disciplinary silos, when what's really needed are teams that treat complex problems spanning mental health, social health, and physical health. In fact, we know that the solution to the rising national bill for healthcare is to solve the problem of complex care: the 5 percent of patients who account for 50 percent of the cost of healthcare in the United States are most often in need of complex care.

This chapter looks at the revolutionaries who can lead America's great academic health institutions, with digital technology companies envisioning consumer-based healthcare delivery. More of us can join the revolution—if we embrace it and the role of leadership in making it happen.

This chapter also suggests that hope is not a strategy, as legacy institutions face the need to become nimble and consumer focused and decide how to meet consumers where they are.

THE CEO AS CHIEF CONSUMER OFFICER

Today's CEOs face the same concerns the public faces—partisan divides that mean any election could switch healthcare policy overnight. We are living in the twilight zone between value-based payments and fee-for-service.

But what remains true is that regardless of how a hospital is reimbursed, it must develop into a consumer-facing institution that creates loyalty by eliminating the fragmentation and confusion felt so often by patients. As a result, a CEO must become an institution's guide to a new future by elevating innovation as a mission, encouraging creativity as a core value, and building the data capacity that allows design thinking to succeed.

A CEO's job, of course, starts with her trustees. Every leader needs a strong, courageous board. It takes a bold group of trustees today to look beyond the obvious accounting measures of revenue over expenses and instead look at investment in the future, culture change, innovation, and commitment to the community.

Healthcare trustees must appreciate and act on the balance between the old math and the emerging new math. Academic medical centers have relied on a traditional formula of patient care collections, tuition and fees, and sometimes research grants.

This isn't "bad" math. But it is under enormous pressure because of the inability to charge patients more, or charge students more. At the same time, federal funding for research is growing, but at smaller increments and with concomitant investment by the institution to grow it. In contrast, the new math includes innovative partnerships to build a consumer platform, as well as an expanded relationship with the community expressed in philanthropy. There isn't a shortage of money from donors; there is a shortage of bold ideas that will pay off in social change. As the industry shifts from traditional charity, donors—the new donors—will want to see results. Both partners and donors want one thing: genuine change.

Jaan Sidorov, MD, argues for harnessing the small-group dynamic of generative wisdom by leading trustees through "problem-based learning sessions," borrowing from medical education's success with problem-based learning. Sidorov (2016) wrote:

> Truly insightful boardroom meetings are still the result of an alchemy that is difficult to create on-demand. When complicated issues arise, every process and skill . . . is still no guarantee against resorting to obsolete heuristics, circular reasoning, over-attention to detail, or dominance by a strong-willed individual. . . . that fails to recognize a new value proposition or misses an emerging enterprise risk.

The wisdom of groups can work. It requires trustees willing to commit to a future-facing strategy in which money invested in an integrated consumer-facing platform becomes preeminent, and where CEOs are held accountable for progress in addressing community needs. The leader has to make sense of what is happening—indeed, he has to bring to life a growth-affirming innovation narrative.

George Day and Greg Shea (2019) of the Wharton School of Economics argue that four levers are most effective for leaders in healthcare.

First, those actions start, of course, by investing in people: creating a leadership academy and hiring team leaders and project directors who value innovation. An organization needs so-called changemakers, individuals who see an opportunity or obstacle and have the gravitas and support to enlist others to follow their lead and look at creative and flexible means to overcome the obstacle or embrace the opportunity.

Formal leadership training works. It starts with self-awareness and builds to seeing how to be effective in changing an organization. It works especially well when it targets mid-career professionals, people who have learned some ropes and are ready to be insiders in the revolution. Pay attention to good people who are uncomfortable with the status quo. Do not dismiss their complaints. They will show you the future.

The second lever, according to Day and Shea, is to encourage prudent risk-taking. The boss who punishes a bad idea creates an organization averse to creativity.

The third lever is to adopt a customer-centric innovation process: build the data sets you need to treat individuals as customers. Doing so may involve a much deeper dive into strategically gathered information about your current and prospective customers.

Fourth, align metrics to innovation: reward learning over scorekeeping.

These four levers speak to a critical need in the pursuit of innovation: invest in building an in-house capability to generate and maintain deep data sets into the interactions between the institution and its customers. These data are key to decision-making at every level, from the handling of test results to the making of appointments.

CHANGING THE DNA OF HEALTHCARE

The educational pipeline also must change. Several universities, and health systems that have sponsored new medical schools, realize that we must change the DNA of healthcare delivery itself—we need students prepared for the age of artificial intelligence and ready to deliver value to communities.

Medical education remains trapped between two historic standardized tests, forcing students to compete for relative advantage based on their ability to succeed at test-taking. Using MCAT scores predisposes medical schools to select, unfortunately, relatively privileged individuals whose greatest skill is sitting alone and absorbing data. But admissions committees are also trapped: Because the Step One board examinations determine whether a student will be accepted to a prestigious residency, admissions committees often argue that accepting students who do poorly on the MCAT is a false promise because they will likely do poorly on the Step One examinations and be unable to pursue the specialty of their choice.

However, some medical schools have fought the trap. They are using emotional intelligence, leadership, and empathy as criteria to select more diverse students. Boston University has been a leader in using holistic admissions to double diversity in its medical school. According to Witzburg and Sondheimer (2013), "Students from groups underrepresented in medicine now make up approximately 20% of the entering class, as compared with 11 to 12% before the adoption of holistic review."

Other schools have used emotional intelligence and leadership skills as criteria twinned to a curriculum that supports them. Thomas Jefferson University pioneered the Jefferson Scale of Empathy, with decades of sustained data supporting it, and which many believe should be an admissions criterion for health professional schools.

In fact, it is time to question whether the "one-size-fits-all" medical education model continues to serve society in light of the fact that it can easily take one individual until she is older than 30 years to finish.

On the one hand, we need physician scientists who can manipulate cells at the back of the eye to stop an aggressive cancer. At the same time, we desperately need physicians with the maturity and emotional intelligence who can earn the trust of their communities to convince a patient to undergo an early eye examination, before the cancer becomes uncurable.

The traditional focus on memorizing information must end. Within a few years, it will be absurd to select medical students based on memorization skills, multiple-choice test results, and organic chemistry grades, which fail to create physicians who are empathetic, communicative, and creative. Tomorrow's physicians will have some type of artificial intelligence next to them that will be better than any human at memorizing the myriad genomic and scientific formulas. What that artificial brain cannot do, however, is *be* human. We need medical students prepared to answer when a patient asks, "What does this mean, doctor?"

Perhaps the most pressing crisis in healthcare is the inability of the workforce to handle complex care. In the current healthcare environment, providers in siloed disciplines and departments treat a costly group of patients who may have multiple chronic illnesses, coupled with learning disabilities, mental health issues, and social or economic challenges. The solution requires schools to collaborate even beyond today's interdisciplinary education to create true community laboratories that develop research-based curricula and build teams for treating complex care. Those who study complex care report that simple solutions can unravel complex problems. But today's reimbursement models don't pay for simple solutions, creating a cycle of high costs as patients seek routine help from the emergency department. For example, at Jefferson Health, a concept called "hotspotting" (https://hotspotting.camdenhealth.org) has been deployed whereby medical students and nursing students communicate with the 5 percent of patients with chronic illnesses who utilize the most resources. In many cases, these efforts have resulted in the trifecta of increased patient satisfaction and better outcomes at a fraction of the cost of emergency department and physician visits.

ANCHOR INSTITUTIONS: A FALSE PROMISE?

The failure to integrate mental, physical, and social health points to a more acute issue: the false promise of "anchor institutions." Many cities, such as Chicago, Baltimore, and Philadelphia, boast of their "eds and meds," and each is rich with historic academic health centers and universities. But each of these cities also ranks among the nation's worst in the longevity gap between zip codes—more than 20 years between their richest and poorest neighborhoods. The consumer revolution must cut across income levels.

The ideas of population health, including addressing the social and economic determinants of health, have not yet taken hold through the academic medical continuum, from selection and training to research and clinical practice. DeVoe and colleagues (2017) issued a call for action to academic medicine:

> To build world-class, 21st-century infrastructure for improving health, [academic medical centers] can renew investments in primary care, strengthen ties with public health, create sustainable community laboratories and classrooms, envision multidisciplinary research centers, and build strong community–academic partnerships for facilitating bidirectional teaching, learning, innovation, and discovery.

EMBRACING DIGITAL HEALTH TECHNOLOGY

We overestimate technology in the short run, but underestimate it in the long run. Nowhere is this more true than in healthcare delivery. It turns out that when a traditional medical center partners with a Silicon Valley firm, medical outcomes can actually improve. Sometimes dramatically.

One key conundrum for healthcare delivery involves type 2 diabetes. Occasionally an individual with this disease has an acute issue requiring great scientific knowledge. However, for the majority of encounters, the science is not remote: Weight and age have overwhelmed the body's ability to handle glucose, and the resulting inflammation attacks every organ. The difficulty lies in helping that individual with sustained complex care—the physical sequelae of the disease, the depression that accompanies it, and the struggles arising from any plan to lose weight consistently without surgery. The social complications are immense: depression can lead to job loss, which leads to a loss of insurance, and so forth.

But a Silicon Valley company, Livongo, founded by people who themselves have diabetes, had an immediate impact on members' hospitalization and emergency department visits, resulting in a dramatic drop in acute care encounters (see the case study on Jefferson Health in chapter 7 for more information).

The lessons learned from digital health firms are many:

- In many instances, the data gathered by our current electronic health records are insufficient to help individuals maintain a healthy lifestyle at home. They do their job— record medical encounters—but they don't provide the knowledge needed by the patient.

- Constant contact through an electronic concierge works. However, we do not yet have a system for patients that even parallels the continuous monitoring of automobiles sitting in garages. In the near future, wearables, robots, and artificial intelligence will constantly monitor vital signs and other parameters and notify you and your caregiver when there is a need for intervention. The static snapshot approach to electronic health records in the physician's office will be replaced by 24/7 monitoring, with information transmitted through phones, voice assistants, and so forth.

- Some companies have found that patients prefer to "talk" to a computer about mental health issues rather than visit a therapist, and, as a result, they can obtain help anytime, anywhere. This change will be especially relevant for younger patients who often relate better to "bots" than humans, particularly about sensitive issues and if the "bot" looks more like them than the human.

Machine learning is not a gimmick in healthcare, although its early applications seem to be little more than toys. But technology's potential to monitor thousands of individuals at once, and to provide real-time help and guidance, is unparalleled. For problems such as heart disease, diabetes, depression, and even compliance with cancer care, using machine learning to help patients can create major breakthroughs in medical outcomes themselves.

THE SWITCH FROM PATIENT TO CONSUMER: GAINING HUMAN UNDERSTANDING

From changing the DNA of healthcare to embracing digital health technology, the CEO as chief consumer officer must finally explore the connection between leadership and the human experience of healthcare: a personal journey of which providers are the guardians. NRC Health defines human understanding within the context of healthcare as providers' ability to understand the people they care for with greater clarity, immediacy, and depth, as well as to appreciate what matters most to each patient to ease her journey. Human understanding encompasses the Picker dimensions and has a deeper purpose—to view patients as more than stakeholders, target audiences, and populations—to know patients as *humans*. The following is an exploration of these three aspects of human understanding.

1. Clarity involves the ability to illuminate the critical moments to improve the patient's treatment(s), outcome(s), and overall experience.

2. Immediacy is the ability to capture what people think and feel about their care in real time and over time, to enable providers to build on what is working and resolve problems with greater speed and personalization.

3. Depth explores a patient's experience through a multidimensional lens. A provider must understand the totality of his interaction with every patient—before, during, and after care—to comprehend the patient's personal journey toward well-being.

These capabilities can be achieved through sophisticated data collection and real-time reporting mechanisms, including transparent reporting of physician performance to the physicians themselves, collection of intelligence about the local market such as community perceptions and preferences, and competitive analysis. Also necessary are outreach, coaching, and comprehensive improvement plans for midlevel managers and frontline staff. However, the most important piece of the puzzle is building a consumer-centric culture, where everyone in a provider organization lives and breathes human understanding. Accomplishing this requires strong messaging and support of these efforts (by means of leadership encouragement and guidance, resource investment, and staff development) by executive leaders and, ultimately, the board.

With human understanding as the ultimate aim, healthcare leaders can go beyond patient-centered care to strategically address the consumer revolution, which will improve our ability to help many more patients. The revolution will fuel performance improvement in healthcare, just as it has in other industries, by transforming this illogical system from one that is confusing, fragmented, tedious, and inequitable to one that meets consumers where they are and is grounded in the *human* at its center.

REFERENCES

Day, G. S., and G. P. Shea. 2019. "Grow Faster by Changing Your Innovation Narrative." *MIT Sloan Management Review*. Published December 10. https://sloanreview.mit.edu/article/grow-faster-by-changing-your-innovation-narrative/.

DeVoe, J. E., S. Likumahuwa-Ackman, J. Shannon, and E. S. Hayward. 2017. "Creating 21st-Century Laboratories and Classrooms for Improving Population Health: A Call to Action for Academic Medical Centers." *Academic Medicine* 92 (4): 475–82.

Sidorov, J. 2016. "Using Problem-Based Wisdom to Transform Governance Oversight to Insight." *Healthcare Transformation* 1 (3): 154–63.

Witzburg, R. A., and H. M. Sondheimer. 2013. "Holistic Review—Shaping the Medical Profession One Applicant at a Time." *New England Journal of Medicine* 368 (17): 1565–67.

CHAPTER 9

Internal Talent Needs

To push healthcare to new heights and achieve the bold proposition of human understanding, consumer-centric leadership is only the beginning. Far beyond the C-suite, within the sprawling halls of the average hospital, hundreds, if not thousands, of feet are on the ground (our potential insider revolutionaries): nurses, physicians, physicians' assistants, nurse practitioners, midwives, security guards, janitors, volunteers, and so forth. These employees are the testing ground for any vision or strategy, and success or failure depends on them.

Engaging employees is far from easy. Across all industries, US worker satisfaction has remained relatively low in the years since the Great Recession. In 2015, satisfaction hit a 10-year high of 49 percent (Weber 2016). The biggest gripe among workers inside and outside of healthcare is being overworked and underpaid.

An engaged employee is in such demand (more than 4,800 hospitals and health systems across the country, plus countless other types of healthcare corporations, are seeking practitioners), an entire industry has sprouted solely to help organizations engage their employees. However, accomplishing this may be difficult without truly defining what is meant by an engaged individual.

> *Employee engagement* is the emotional commitment the employee has to the organization and its goals.

This emotional commitment means engaged employees actually care about their work and their company. They don't just work for a paycheck or for the next promotion, but work on behalf of the organization's goals, which they share (Kruse 2012).

What if we took a step back and looked at what it means to be an engaged individual in society? For that, we turn to Abraham Maslow, an American psychologist who studied human needs. He devised a hierarchy, an ascending level of needs from the most basic to the most desirable and difficult to attain. These rungs are sometimes referred to as "Maslow's Mountain" because, much like climbing a real mountain, it can be difficult, if not impossible, for many to reach the top (see exhibit 9.1).

Most of us take for granted our basic physical needs such as food and water until we are faced with situations in which we are deprived of them. As we move up the mountain, our needs become more emotional. Not everyone has friends or feels a sense of connection. Many who do still lack self-esteem or don't feel recognized by others in their lives. The summit is self-actualization.

EXHIBIT 9.1: Maslow's Hierarchy

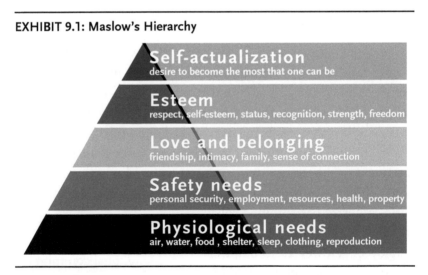

Source: McLeod (2018).

This, Maslow argued, is the fulfillment of one's purpose. It's also incredibly rare for one to achieve sustained self-actualization.

Where does work come into play in this hierarchy? Surely, as overworked Americans, we find some connection between our needs and our jobs. In chapter 5, we discussed the calling of healthcare and the emotional connection many caregivers feel toward their work. But do we gain friendships, self-respect, and even self-actualization in our jobs?

COMPASSION FATIGUE

No industry puts an emotional strain on its workers quite like healthcare. Like other industries, healthcare has plenty of unengaged employees. But lack of engagement can be much more dangerous in healthcare. For example, nurse engagement is the number one variable correlating to patient mortality, more than the nurse-to-patient ratio (Aiken et al. 2002). Disengaged employees call in sick more often, pay less attention when they are at work, and tend to leave their jobs faster, causing higher staff turnover. Healthcare is already facing worker shortages, and an emergency department that is understaffed or staffed with distracted, detached workers is a recipe for disaster.

Compassion fatigue is defined as the "physical and mental exhaustion and emotional withdrawal experienced by those who care for sick or traumatized people over an extended period of time" (Merriam-Webster 2020). In healthcare, compassion fatigue is an issue for all members of the care team. Physicians suffer from burnout in especially high numbers, according to one study designed to provide a representative snapshot of physicians and the general US working population (Sternberg 2016). Nearly half of physicians (49 percent) meet the definition for overall burnout, compared with 28 percent of other US workers. A more detailed analysis revealed that more than 54 percent of physicians have at least one symptom of burnout (Alexander and Ballou 2018). Emotional exhaustion and depersonalization among physicians is also more than one-and-a-half times greater than among the general working population. Physicians work a median of 50 hours per week, and their satisfaction with the work–life balance is far lower than that of other workers: 36 percent versus approximately 66 percent (Comparably 2020; Westgate 2014). Researchers in another study found that increasing a nurse's workload by one surgical patient was associated with a 7 percent increase in a patient's odds of dying within 30 days of admission. Boosting the workload from four to six patients resulted in a 14 percent increase in a patient's risk of dying, while increasing the workload from six to eight patients resulted in a 31 percent increase in the risk of dying (Ball et al. 2018).

According to a survey of nearly 8,000 surgeons published in the *Annals of Surgery*, 9 percent of respondents stated that they had made a major medical error in the past three months. Approximately 70 percent attributed these perceived errors to a personal issue such as fatigue, stress, or a lapse in judgment. The worse the surgeon's burnout, the more likely he was to report having made a medical error. Specifically, each 1-point increase in a surgeon's score on a scale of emotional exhaustion was associated with a 5 percent increase in the odds of having reported an error, while a 1-point increase in a surgeon's depersonalization score was tied to an 11 percent increase (Shanafelt et al. 2010).

These findings point to the need to pay attention to employee engagement all the way to the top of the organization. Hiring, helping, and proactively retaining employees should be on every hospital CEO's short list of priorities. However, just 26 percent of organizational leaders said employee engagement is "very important" (Dale Carnegie & Associates 2018). The same survey also found that 31 percent of managers strongly agreed that their companies make employee engagement a top priority, while 16 percent "somewhat or strongly disagreed." Yet, 41 percent of senior leaders strongly agreed they are supporting their managers in efforts to engage employees, and only 8 percent disagreed. Clearly, senior leaders believe they are supporting employee engagement more than do their direct reports. This gap could be one reason for the disconnect among employees on the ground.

One common myth is that healthcare is a bustling, growth-generating industry that naturally pays well and therefore has higher employee engagement. In the context of work, does money buy happiness? Princeton University researchers studied this connection and found a link between an increase in salary and an increase in engagement; however, they found that every 1 percent increase in employee satisfaction required a 10 percent increase in salary (Kahneman and Deaton 2010). This one-to-ten ratio means that hefty raises would be required to even modestly boost employee satisfaction. While money certainly isn't unimportant, it doesn't seem to hold the key to an engaged healthcare workforce.

MEASUREMENT

How then can we boost employee engagement in healthcare? Nearly every hospital and health system conducts annual engagement surveys, and the results of these surveys flood into human resources departments. Many of these surveys are long: Every department has questions to include, and often there is a stack of legacy questions that cannot be abandoned for fear of severing a trend on an important issue. The result is a deluge of data for human resource managers to comb through and analyze in order to find actionable results. To say their backs are against the wall is an understatement. NRC Health's employee engagement study provides additional context (see exhibit 9.2).

Another issue is data integration—comparing and sharing the perspectives of employees and patients to reveal areas of strength and opportunity as well as to identify deeper issues that may threaten the organization in ways that are not readily apparent.

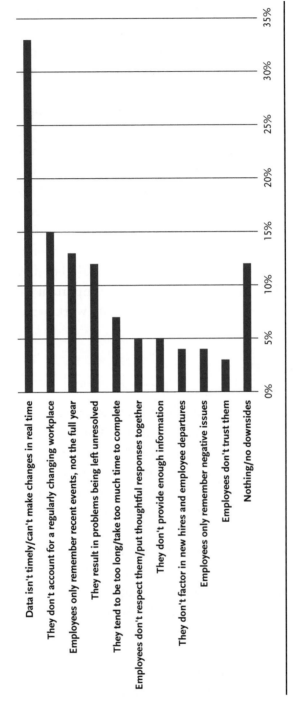

EXHIBIT 9.2: Reasons Managers Give for Dissatisfaction with Annual Employee Surveys

Source: NRC Health (2018).

INTERNAL NET PROMOTER SCORE

The net promoter score (NPS), a staple of measuring loyalty in business, asks people to rate an organization based on their likelihood to recommend its products or services to family and friends. The idea is that people will only recommend an organization if they are committed to the organization themselves. When we zoom in on employees in particular, their loyalty to the organization that employs them becomes an even more important litmus test as to how they feel about their employer. According to NRC Health's employee engagement studies (NRC Health 2018), large swaths of healthcare workers are not advocates for their organization. On a standard 11-point NPS scale, only 32 percent of employees were engaged (a score of 9 or 10), while 29 percent were disengaged (a score of 0 to 6). The largest segment of employees—38 percent—had a score of 7 or 8 and were considered passive. If we calculated an NPS for the average healthcare organization, it would receive a paltry 3 out of a possible 100, a very similar score to that for the average cable company (see exhibit 9.3).

The same NPS structured question was asked of healthcare employees in terms of the organization and specifically how it

EXHIBIT 9.3: Average Net Promoter Score for Hospitals and Health Systems by Employees

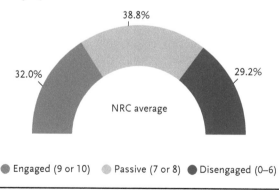

38.8%

32.0%

29.2%

NRC average

● Engaged (9 or 10) ● Passive (7 or 8) ● Disengaged (0–6)

Source: NRC Health (2018).

delivers on the patient experience. Are organizations ready to engage their patients? The results were only slightly better than those for employee engagement: 41 percent of employees gave their organization a score of 9 or 10 on engagement, 21 percent reported that the organization was disengaged (a score of 0 to 6), and 37 percent stated that it was passive (a score of 7 or 8) (see exhibit 9.4).

These numbers reveal a problem inside the healthcare organization and in the minds of employees. We often don't believe in ourselves enough to deliver excellent patient care. If we can't engage our own employees, how do we hope to engage patients and consumers who will be our future patients?

Interestingly, healthcare employees and healthcare consumers are on common ground here. Both groups set a high bar for how healthcare should be, and neither feels like it is measuring up. When was the last time we tried to compare employee and consumer perspectives? We usually keep them separate within our many silos. Employee research is housed within human resources, and consumer research is housed within the marketing department. Both departments spend plenty of time researching their respective audiences, but never the twain shall meet.

EXHIBIT 9.4: Net Promoter Score for Organizational Engagement by Employees

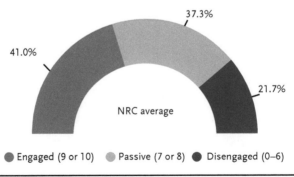

Source: NRC Health (2018).

EMPLOYEE EXPERIENCE + CONSUMER EXPERIENCE

We know this much: When employees are engaged, they deliver a better patient experience. And when employees aren't engaged, it's not just human resources' problem. Patient experiences suffer from disengaged employees, and patients are well aware when a decline in employee engagement occurs (see exhibit 9.5).

Thus, increasing employee engagement becomes a patient-centered imperative. For the past decade, NRC Health has been diligently tracking the organizations that are trying to improve employee engagement while keeping an eye on patient ratings. It's clear that the two move in concert with one another (see exhibit 9.6).

Why don't more organizations tie the two together? Much like the rest of healthcare, each department is incredibly busy and dealing with its own dashboard of metrics—many tied to their paychecks—which keeps the blinders on and prevents collaboration

EXHIBIT 9.5: Organization Engagement and Patient Satisfaction

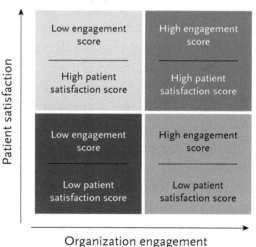

Source: NRC Health (2018).

EXHIBIT 9.6: Patient Ratings Increase with Engagement Ratings

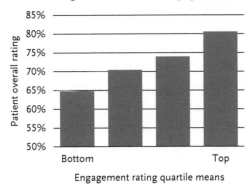

Source: NRC Health (2010–2016).

across departments. However, this type of movement is precisely what is needed to make big changes to an organization and ultimately deliver a patient experience to which everyone is contributing and owning.

As we try to find a way to bring these areas together, we return to the original Picker work and the eight dimensions of care. For a quarter century we generally have thought about these dimensions in terms of patients only. But for the dimensions to be delivered, caregivers must be educated and engaged in each dimension. For "access to care" to be delivered, the person who answers the phone must exhibit a good attitude and a problem-solving approach. For "physical comfort" to be delivered, a caregiver needs to display a human touch and an empathetic ear.

NRC Health has been training employees in Picker's eight dimensions for several years. Most healthcare organizations assume employees know these tactics, but the evidence we present indicates that most either do not know or have forgotten them. Employees often complain of not having enough training and support in the things they *didn't* learn in school.

THE STORY OF UNIVERSITY OF ILLINOIS MEDICAL CENTER

The healthcare industry makes a lot of assumptions about what its employees know. For instance, internal culture and branding efforts are intended to reflect an organization's mission, build a vision for the organization, and instill values in employees that will translate into day-to-day behaviors.

The University of Illinois Medical Center (UIMC) had similar assumptions about its employees when it attempted to build an external brand for consumers. As one of several academic medical centers in Chicago, including the University of Chicago, UIMC was in a challenging position. It is physically located on the campus of the University of Illinois at Chicago and its name was constantly confused with the University of Chicago. Its leaders recognized that internal brand confusion existed, and they sought a way to remedy it.

Most organizations considering a brand refresh hire a creative firm and head straight to the marketing and advertising concepts to spread awareness of the brand and boost their image to consumers. But what about awareness and willingness to recommend among UIMC's own employees? Often, brand messaging flies right over their heads. When an employee sees a brand message for the first time on a billboard in the midst of other commuters, she can be resentful and feel left out.

UIMC wanted to avoid this trap by looking at these two audiences—consumers and employees—together. What if employees were treated like consumers? It seems radical to not assume your employees know your brand inside and out, but the results can be fascinating.

The medical center discovered that many employees lacked knowledge about the brand and struggled to recall basic concepts about the organization's mission, vision, and values. Much like external consumers, they were unable to point out exactly what made the organization different from competitors and had trouble painting a picture of the brand's future direction. Some employees even went so far as to say they may not use UIMC as their provider of choice.

UIMC was open to the results, and the marketing team and branding firm decided to suspend any new external advertising to focus first on employees. An internal branding campaign took shape, with the main goals of first acknowledging that employees didn't know enough about UIMC and then giving them the knowledge and tools to learn more and become brand advocates.

Leaders launched this internal branding campaign with a ribbon-cutting event and through information fairs in which employees could learn about the organization and its benefits, much like a would-be job applicant. They created a robust employee-friendly physician directory and posted additional primary care resources, including extended appointment hours, intended for both internal and external use. Fair organizers also included testimonials so employees could hear from others like themselves about the organization. All events and resources had a strong C-suite presence.

The results were clear: After six months, employees had a knowledge boost and a better understanding of the brand. They were more aware of UIMC's offerings and—just as is the goal with consumers—more likely to choose and recommend UIMC for care in the future (see exhibit 9.7).

By launching an internal branding campaign first, UIMC leaders were able to gather feedback and home in on the right message for external consumers. Once in the market, they saw better results in overall brand awareness among consumers, just as they had with employees. By using employees as a testing ground, they built internal and external brand advocates.

In the end, employee engagement and patient and consumer experiences are linked in virtually every healthcare organization. Clearly, there is room for improvement in engaging both key audiences. However, what predates the experience is the *perception* of the experience. Among employees, this perception pertains to how they feel about their jobs each and every day—if they feel they

EXHIBIT 9.7: Consumer and Employee Decision Models

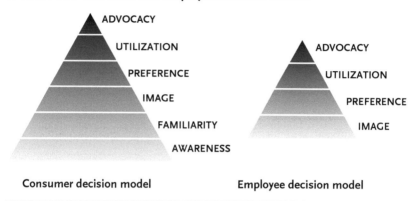

Consumer decision model: ADVOCACY, UTILIZATION, PREFERENCE, IMAGE, FAMILIARITY, AWARENESS

Employee decision model: ADVOCACY, UTILIZATION, PREFERENCE, IMAGE

Source: NRC Health.

can deliver the brand promise while maximizing their talents and achieving fulfillment in their role.

EMPLOYEE ENABLEMENT

The future of employee engagement requires the separation of traditional engagement drivers from the resources that employees desire, but never seem to get. Managers often work within the confines of the employee's role, pay and benefits, interaction with other employees and their roles ("org-charting"), leadership rounding, teamwork, respect and recognition, and development opportunities. These are boilerplate management duties that every employee expects from a manager. Although vital, they are not key to enabling employees to fulfill their potential and climb Maslow's mountain.

What is needed is a separate structure to promote employee empowerment through coaching, additional role resources, expanded training opportunities, collaborative efforts (cross-functional projects), volunteer opportunities, and other off-role responsibilities that employees greatly appreciate (see exhibit 9.8).

For example, employees want their managers to provide career planning and development services, but many managers see career

EXHIBIT 9.8: Improving the Culture: Engagement and Enablement

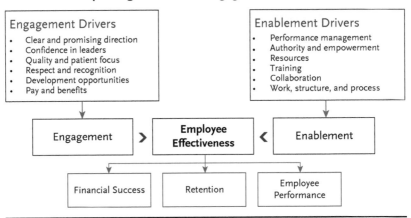

Engagement Drivers
- Clear and promising direction
- Confidence in leaders
- Quality and patient focus
- Respect and recognition
- Development opportunities
- Pay and benefits

Enablement Drivers
- Performance management
- Authority and empowerment
- Resources
- Training
- Collaboration
- Work, structure, and process

Engagement > Employee Effectiveness < Enablement

Financial Success | Retention | Employee Performance

Source: NRC Health (2018).

planning as a threat. They don't want to run a training program for their competition if and when employees are ready to move on. But this reluctance is the opposite of what most employees need. They need help from their managers to envision their future with the organization. The average American spends only one and one-half hours a year on career planning. By comparison, Americans spend an average of 946 hours on leisure activities and sports and 400 hours on household activities. Without support from their employer, employees aren't going to feel as if they have a plan, and when they become disgruntled, they will be more likely to pull the ripcord, leaving healthcare organizations with holes to plug on the organizational chart.

When employers are willing to separate some of these hard and soft responsibilities, they have a better chance of connecting with managers in the job areas that keep them fired up and engaged. For example, if an employee wants to volunteer more and the manager not only allows her to take time off to do so but also inquires about the experience, devotes a few minutes in a team huddle for her to report on it, and extends the offer to volunteer to other direct reports, a feeling is generated among employees that managers aren't just complying with their request but actually care about them when they aren't at work. Employees may notice the increased attention from managers who are truly invested in their future. This, in turn, could create a more driven workforce ready to fulfill their potential in their existing roles and beyond.

When healthcare workforces are mobilized to fulfill their potential, the ultimate beneficiary is the patient. It is impossible to envision patient-centered care without activated and empowered employees who, perhaps, have recaptured the inspiration that brought them to healthcare in the first place.

REFERENCES

Aiken, L. H., S. P. Clarke, D. M. Sloane, J. Sochalski, and J. H. Silber. 2002. "Hospital Nurse Staffing and Patient Mortality, Nurse Burnout, and Job Dissatisfaction." *Journal of the American Medical Association.* Published October 23. https://jamanetwork.com/journals/jama/fullarticle/195438.

Alexander, A. G., and K. A. Ballou. 2018. "Work–Life Balance, Burnout, and the Electronic Health Record." *American Journal of Medicine* 131 (8): 857–58.

Ball, J. E., L. Bruyneel, L. H. Aiken, W. Sermeus, D. M. Sloane, A. M. Rafferty, R. Lindqvist, C. Tishelman, P. Griffiths, and RN4Cast Consortium. 2018. "Post-Operative Mortality, Missed Care and Nurse Staffing in Nine Countries: A Cross-Sectional Study." *International Journal of Nursing Studies* 78: 10–15.

Comparably. 2020. "Survey: Two-Thirds of Employees Are Satisfied with Their Work–Life Balance." Updated January 13. www.comparably.com/news/survey-two-thirds-of-employees-are-satisfied-with-their-work-life-balance/.

Dale Carnegie & Associates. 2018. *Employee Engagement: It's Time to Go All In. Making Engagement a Daily Priority for Leaders.* Accessed February 28, 2020. www.dalecarnegie.com/en/resources/employee-engagement-making-engagement-a-daily-priority-for-leaders.

Kahneman, D., and A. Deaton. 2010. "High Income Improves Evaluation of Life but Not Emotional Well-Being." *Proceedings of the National Academy of Sciences* 107 (38): 16489–93.

Kruse, K. 2012. "What Is Employee Engagement?" *Forbes*. Published June 22. www.forbes.com/sites/kevinkruse/2012/06/22/employee-engagement-what-and-why/.

McLeod, S. 2018. "Maslow's Hierarchy of Needs." *Simply Psychology*. Accessed March 14, 2020. www.simplypsychology.org/maslow.html.

Merriam-Webster. 2020. "Compassion Fatigue." Accessed February 28. www.merriam-webster.com/dictionary/compassionfatigue.

NRC Health. 2010, 2011, 2012, 2013, 2014, 2015, 2016, 2018. *Employee Engagement Studies*. Lincoln, NE: NRC Health.

Shanafelt, T. D., C. M. Balch, G. Bechamps, T. Russell, L. Dyrbye, D. Satele, P. Collicott, P. J. Novotny, J. Sloan, and J. Freischlag. 2010. "Burnout and Medical Errors Among American Surgeons." *Annals of Surgery* 256 (6): 995–1000.

Sternberg, S. 2016. "Diagnosis: Burnout." *U.S. News & World Report*. Published September 8. www.usnews.com/news/articles/2016-09-08/doctors-battle-burnout-to-save-themselves-and-their-patients.

Weber, L. 2016. "Job Satisfaction Hits a 10-Year High—but It's Still Below 50%." *Wall Street Journal*. Published July 19. www.wsj.com/articles/job-satisfaction-hits-a-10-year-highbut-its-still-below-50-1468940401.

Westgate, A. 2014. "Eighteen Work–Life Balance Tips for Physicians." *Physicians Practice*. Published July 30. www.physicianspractice.com/great-american-physician-survey/eighteen-work-life-balance-tips-physicians.

CHAPTER 10

Removing Barriers

ONCE HEALTHCARE ORGANIZATIONS activate and empower employees to recapture their inspiration for human understanding, they have a tremendous opportunity to turn that inward transformation outward to help shape the communities around them. Every neighborhood in the United States leans on the local hospital as a bedrock of the community and a provider of lifesaving care to residents. Once employees are engaged, enabled, and mobilized to live the mission of the organization, the next frontier becomes transforming the patient experience itself through the Picker dimensions. After all, without patients there would be no hospitals, no physicians, no nurses. However, as our research has revealed, far too often the road to patient-centered care is littered with distractions and barriers. These hurdles wear down caregivers and create malaise among employees. No one suffers more from bad care than patients. So what, exactly, keeps getting in the way?

RESPECT FOR PATIENTS' VALUES, PREFERENCES, AND EXPRESSED NEEDS

The mission of healthcare organizations is to serve all who come through the doors, but that means people from different walks of life with different expectations regarding their care. Organizations that want to better understand their consumers must start with a shift on the inside: Staff members must fully understand the different health beliefs and practices among patients, as well as the ethnic and cultural groups in their specific patient population. They need to ask questions of the patient population to better understand their needs and beliefs. Caregivers also need to view and treat patients holistically—mind, body, and soul. Staff members should ask more questions about therapeutic decisions that can affect patients' lives. For example, ask the patient if he prefers to be treated with medication or possibly with alternative therapies. Allowing patients to heal in the way they prefer can result in better outcomes.

Many organizations are starting to provide patients with direct access to their medical records, which allows them to view all the episodes and decisions that make up their care journey. Some top-performing organizations allow patients to interact with their providers through communications protected by the Health Insurance Portability and Accountability Act. Organizations are also providing educational materials in the medical record so patients can conduct their own research by visiting reliable websites and accessing high-quality content about their condition, medications, and side effects.

Other important activities include comprehensive planning and services focused on the particular needs of cultural groups and diagnostic groups. Such personalization can be achieved through virtual or in-person support groups composed of patients with similar conditions and family members or through education (e.g., a nutrition guide for patients with diabetes).

COORDINATION AND INTEGRATION OF CARE

As hospitals have grown into health systems and the front doors to care have multiplied, the confusion patients feel has increased. This confusion is not limited to access but also pertains to the patient experience itself. Consumers often feel their care is uncoordinated and haphazard. When caregivers don't work together in an attempt to integrate a patient's care, this unsettling patient perspective becomes reality. Therefore, caregivers must make a concerted effort to provide coordinated care.

For example, giving patients written and visual information about the members of their care team can create a bond between patient and caregiver. Explaining each caregiver's role and how the caregivers' roles connect around the patient, and identifying the clinician in charge, can fill in a patient's educational gaps and boost her confidence early in the experience.

Many organizations throughout the United States are using team-based care to help with the coordination of patient care. Team-based care enables patients to feel confident that the team is communicating and working together. Similarly, team-based care is effective in the clinic setting when all specialists are in one location for a patient's visit. Rather than needing to go to multiple facilities for treatment, patients can experience streamlined care without challenging transitions.

But what about when things go wrong? While it's always important to stay on top of errors and service gaffes, it's even more important to plan for them. Giving patients and their families realistic expectations about wait times, expected levels of discomfort, possible adverse effects, and other factors germane to care delivery can help staff prepare patients for things that may go awry. A patient who is told at the outset that the provider is running late or that a procedure isn't always perfect will be far less frustrated than a patient who finds out after the fact.

INFORMATION, COMMUNICATION, AND EDUCATION

Information needs to be conveyed via multiple vehicles so it is accessible to all patients. Top-performing organizations use their Patient and Family Advisor Councils to review educational materials and ensure that the content is understandable to patients and families, rather than medical jargon. They also rely on feedback from these councils to ensure that information is communicated in various ways (e.g., video, written materials, support groups). The increasing number of digitally savvy consumers makes it vital to include information in electronic medical records. When patients can review important data while still in the hospital and then review it at home as they get back to daily life, the result can be less friction during the recovery process. Having "to do" items such as reading educational material or watching a video provides patients with reliable information when they go home. Most patients don't feel they have enough information when they are discharged.

Beyond individual patient interactions, healthcare organizations must determine how they can systematize education across their patient population. Educational workshops for all staff members—including employed physicians—can result in improved communication with all patients. These workshops often involve role-playing and action planning with an emphasis on how to combat the most common challenges that patients face. To be most effective, these workshops must draw on actual patient feedback.

Asking patients about their health-related goals—the "why" behind wanting to get better—is vital to providing the right information at the right time. Does a patient want to attend his son's wedding? The conversation might shift to when the patient may be able to travel again or gain full mobility. Does a patient want to ride horses again? If so, the conversation might shift to risks involved if further injury occurs. These conversations provide realistic expectations, a reasonable timeline, and a better understanding of what may happen once a patient leaves the hospital.

More and more organizations are focusing on population health issues. When doing this, they are essentially writing "wellness prescriptions." These prescriptions allow for an organization to list nutritional guidelines and the exercise the patient needs to maintain when leaving the hospital. Organizations are also evaluating patients in terms of food insecurities and providing food prescriptions for their food pharmacy. They understand that if the patient does not have food to eat in the future, she will not take a medication that must be taken with food. Another potential question is to ask patients if they have working electricity in their home; if a medication needs to be refrigerated, does the patient have a way to keep it cold? Healthcare organizations are asking patients with asthma if they have clean, properly filtered air in the home, and, if not, they are working with social service agencies to help find solutions.

PHYSICAL COMFORT

Among all patient needs, perhaps none is more basic than physical comfort. There is nothing worse than being unable to sleep in the hospital because of constant interruptions and distractions. Hospitals can be quite uncomfortable. Scheduling the many routine but necessary procedures—blood draws, regular doses of medication, bathing, weighing, daily radiographs, and so forth—can mean long days and nights for patients, and longer checklists for caregivers. However, striving to schedule these tasks during waking hours and allowing patients to rest as much as possible at night is vital. Little acts of thoughtfulness such as providing shelf space and bulletin boards in patients' rooms to permit them to personalize their space can mean a world of difference. Keeping patients comfortable and safe should be on every checklist.

Healthcare organizations can also enhance physical comfort by furnishing waiting areas with movable tables, chairs, and sofas to allow visitors to create their own comfort zones. Many organizations now have multiple waiting areas with different types of furniture to suit visitors' varying preferences. Televisions and areas for laptop use also add convenience and comfort to waiting areas.

EMOTIONAL SUPPORT AND ALLEVIATION OF FEAR AND ANXIETY

The patient journey can be one of the most emotionally taxing experiences of a person's life. Just as an emotional connection is vital to employees delivering on an organizational mission, it is essential for caregivers to acknowledge the emotional needs of patients and to nurture them. But they shouldn't have to do this alone. Healthcare organizations can develop a network of patients and family members willing to share their experiences with newly diagnosed patients and their families. Top-performing organizations provide support groups for patients as well as for staff and managers, closing an important feedback loop of internal and external emotional support. For example, a staff member diagnosed with cancer can attend a support group as a patient, but he can also be part of a support group whose aim is to understand what it means to be a caregiver with cancer. Support groups are also available for managers who have staff members with cancer so they can better support them, personally and professionally, on their journey.

Creating customized experiences also helps the patient heal. Ask the patient about something she enjoys or a nickname she likes to be called. If the patient loves a certain college football team, for example, a staff member can note this in the chart, and caregivers can mention the score of a recent game when they come into the patient's room.

Some organizations are relying more on volunteers to help ease patients' anxiety. Volunteers can sit with anxious patients in the waiting room to help calm their nerves. If a provider knows a particular patient tends to be nervous when coming to the office, this is a perfect opportunity for a volunteer to provide emotional support for the patient in the waiting area (Institute for Healthcare Improvement and NRC Health 2019).

INVOLVEMENT OF FAMILY AND FRIENDS

We have mentioned family and friends in several chapters, but this is an aspect of the patient experience that, surprisingly, can be easy to ignore. Family and friends can make a crucial difference to patients as they receive care and are on the road to recovery. To that end, healthcare organizations need to have respite rooms for families so they can remain in the facility while their loved one receives care. Family members may not want to be far from the patient, but they also need rest in order to care for the patient when he returns home. Caregivers must make sure the family knows where the respite rooms are located.

Ask the patient who will be her caregiver. Then, when staff members are having important conversations with the patient, make sure this caregiver is present. If the caregiver is not present, a staff member should ask if there is a more convenient time for the caregiver to attend or provide a line for him to call in and receive updates about the patient. Alternatively, provide an email address or a website URL that will enable the caregiver to transmit a message via an online portal (many organizations are now providing a physical or virtual space for family members to leave questions). Access to an online portal or to a whiteboard in a patient's room also allows family members to write down questions, which can be particularly helpful if they forgot to inquire about something during a meeting with the care team.

Family members also like to connect with family members of other patients in the hospital. One way for these families to connect is through a nonalcoholic "happy hour," which enables them to establish their own informal support network. Some organizations also ask volunteers to bring fresh baked cookies one day a week to a certain floor. Not only will patients and families want to stop by, but staff members look forward to connecting with volunteers and family members. When healthcare organizations are responsive to the needs of family and friends, their power to heal the patient becomes even stronger.

CONTINUITY AND TRANSITION

The actual patient care journey is rarely as flawless as depicted in PowerPoint presentations at healthcare conferences or on websites of healthcare providers. As we discussed in chapters 3 and 4, most consumers are plagued by disjointed experiences and confusion at every turn. Even if they work for a hospital, consumers often begin a healthcare journey without enough information to confidently navigate their care. It is easy to pin this lack of education on the consumer, but healthcare's complexity poses a challenge for patients with varying degrees of knowledge about the industry. Hospitals and their employees must bridge the complexity gap and provide coordinated patient care, which starts with human-to-human interaction and education.

As noted previously, the patient must have a designated caregiver at the outset of the care journey. Top-performing organizations integrate this person into all essential components of the care journey, including conversations about medications and what to expect when going home. If the patient needs physical therapy when transitioning home, the hospital ensures that the designated caregiver is present for the exercise education so she will know how to assist the patient and recognize when the exercise is done correctly or not.

Begin discharge education during admissions by providing important information on the intake form. Nurses can then discuss relevant discharge details throughout the patient's hospital stay to enhance understanding and set expectations (e.g., present some of the acronyms the patient may hear and explain what they mean, as they will be part of the care plan to ensure he is healing and able to go home). Bedside educators are trained to make sure that patients understand all of their conversations with and instructions from nurses and physicians. If they do not understand something, the educator rephrases the information to ensure a smooth discharge process (Zablocki 2015).

Because patients have different needs, the organization should consider distributing customized discharge instructions including a copy of the discharge summary, medication cards, educational videos of the discharge process, and any other videos that might be beneficial to the patient back at home. Give patients a chance to ask any final questions and make sure they don't walk out of the building until all of their questions and concerns have been addressed.

Finally, don't let patients drive away without reaching out. Like an attentive waiter who makes sure the customer is satisfied with his meal, the organization should schedule phone calls within the first day or two after discharge to ensure that the transition home goes as expected and all questions have been answered. If nurses or other caregivers are too busy to call, consider setting up an automated system to ensure no patients are left out.

ACCESS TO CARE

Before patients ever walk through one of our doors, they are increasingly likely to find us through a screen—a cell phone, tablet, computer, or other convenient device. As a result, healthcare organizations must be proactive and provide information and access to care where the consumer wants it, not necessarily where it is convenient for the provider. Doing so starts with being transparent about provider reviews and comments, as well as posting educational materials about various conditions on the organization's website. Consumers are turning to Google and accessing WebMD regularly to research their own conditions. Providing reliable educational materials allows the health system to share the knowledge the consumer is seeking; in turn, she is highly likely to seek care at your institution because she views it as the expert on her condition. Ignoring patients' digital first steps can limit a healthcare organization's ability to influence patients and start the patient journey on the right foot.

Healthcare organizations must be increasingly "off campus" and more involved in the community so that consumers recognize the brand in their daily lives and not just when they are sick. Offering telehealth services to school nursing offices initiates a partnership from the beginning. If a sick child is in the nurse's office, the nurse may conduct telemedicine if the parent signed onto this program when registering the child for school. Doing so allows the child to receive a visit with his physician while in the school nurse's office. When the parent picks the child up, the provider has already phoned in any needed prescriptions, relieving the parent of the need to take the child in for care, wait for the appointment, and then wait for the prescription to be called in to the pharmacy and filled. This convenience can make a big difference to patients and families as they ponder their accessibility to the care they need.

ADDRESSING COMPASSION FATIGUE

We can remove all of the above barriers and improve the patient experience across the board, as long as our caregivers are up to the challenge. But what happens when a nurse is drained of the ability to be nice or a physician can no longer answer another question? What happens when the spirit that drove a caregiver into medicine in the first place seems to be getting crushed? (For a discussion of compassion fatigue, see chapter 9.)

How do organizations resolve this issue? According to NRC Health's Physician Engagement National Survey, conducted from 2015 to 2017, physicians want to spend more time with their patients. They want to be sure that their patient loads are not so heavy that they do not have enough time to fully discuss the patient's medical condition, necessary tests, and treatment options with the patient and family members. Creating more team-based care is important to physicians to enable better communication throughout the care team and organization. Physicians also want more rigorous systems of checks and balances to prevent medical errors in the hospital. Moreover, they like to work for organizations that keep up with the latest advancements in medical equipment and technology.

One way to combat physician caregiver fatigue is to assign a mentor—someone the physician can trust, develop a rapport with, and contact when he is struggling.

Many top organizations conduct rounds on their staff, and effective staff rounds have been shown to help combat compassion fatigue (Thompson 2013). Staff rounds enable leaders to make sure that staff members have everything they need from a clinical standpoint to do their job, as well as a manageable workload. Staff members understand that there will be times of high census, but this is when it is crucial to provide extra recognition for those who go above and beyond in their day-to-day duties.

Keep in mind that things sometimes go wrong in healthcare, and those incidents can be a matter of life or death. Healthcare organizations must provide a safe space for staff members to grieve when they lose a patient. Many organizations have a code that when called allows for food or something soothing to be brought to the care team to comfort them and give them a moment to grieve. Quiet rooms are also available for staff members to use when a patient dies or when they need to recharge. Some organizations hold monthly sessions for hospital staff to discuss what went well and what went wrong with difficult cases. In addition to the medical issues, staff members discuss the emotional impact of the case, so they all can share in the experience.

Patient- and family-centered care week is another activity many hospitals and health systems offer. During this week, former patients and family members share their stories. They tell staff members how much they affected their lives and that they will always remember them. Such words of appreciation help recharge caregivers when they need it the most.

Recognizing staff throughout the year for exemplary service is important. However, if employees are only recognized for improvement, the result can be a vicious boom-and-bust cycle of improvement.

BREAKING THE CYCLE OF IMPROVEMENT

In healthcare, improvement is a marathon, not a sprint. If too much emphasis is placed on improvement, and leadership becomes infatuated with boosting scores, the result can be similar to compassion fatigue. By its nature, sustainable improvement must be slow and steady. Rapid jumps in scores are difficult to sustain, and scores that go up and down too much can create frustration, and even apathy, regarding the pursuit of improvement.

Leaders in top organizations are aware of this pitfall and support a methodical and measured approach to improvement that enables the hospital to avoid boom-and-bust cycles and improvement apathy. By shifting the conversation from "How does this impact the bottom line?" to "How does this impact the consumer's experience?" healthcare providers can ensure they are implementing initiatives that have a positive impact on patients, families, consumers, and caregivers; maintain focus on the mission and on the patient; and ultimately overcome the barriers described in this chapter.

REFERENCES

Institute for Healthcare Improvement and NRC Health. 2019. *Mass Customization in Healthcare Delivery.* Webinar. Presented July 1.

Thompson, A. 2013. "How Schwartz Rounds Can Be Used to Combat Compassion Fatigue." *Nursing Management* 20 (4): 16–20.

Zablocki, E. 2015. *Bryan Health Educates Patients One Discharge at a Time (Part One)*. Picker Institute Patient-Centered Care case study. NRC Health. Published July. https://nrchealth.com/wp-content/uploads/2016/10/CS_Bryan-Health-Part-One.pdf.

CHAPTER 11

Nonpreferred and Preferred Future

ECONOMISTS USE HARD measures of reality to poke holes in our views of a utopian healthcare system. The problem, of course, is when they're right. If you ask a health economist to predict American healthcare delivery in ten years, she will remind you of some hard numbers. The cost of care to the nation is rising as a percentage of gross domestic product. Within states' budgets, spending on healthcare rises in proportion to a decline in expenditures for education: Healthcare is the Pac-Man that is eating the budget.

And most importantly, by many measures, the United States continues to have a separate system for the wealthy and one for the poor, with fewer middle-class people feeling secure in their insurance plans.

This is perhaps the most brutal reality, and there is an urgent need to solve health disparities. But looking at America's major cities, now home to 50 percent of the population, we find gaps in longevity based on zip code that are among the worst in the world. In a country as wealthy as ours, it is an indictment on the entire healthcare system that one's zip code is more important than one's genetic code.

This book focuses on the very real, and very needed, consumer revolution. And it is not just about the technology. The key will be how we use these new technologies and digital transformations to not only benefit those who can afford fancy electronics, but also those who are the most vulnerable because of social and socioeconomic factors. So let's look backward in time, and then forward, to seek some answers to crafting a new future.

If we were writing this book 30 years ago—back when physicians blamed managed care for burnout, we might have asked three questions:

1. There seems to be a huge problem with health inequities, both in American cities and around the globe. Why can't we address them?
2. Physicians seem to respond poorly to change and often want to accept the status quo. How do we get physicians to be more creative, adaptable, and optimistic about a changing future?
3. My bank just got an ATM. Why can't healthcare do cool consumer things like that?

Those same questions could be asked today. Health inequities are just as serious; physicians are still afraid to change; and although you can now do all your holiday shopping online, if you have a stomachache, in all likelihood you are getting on the phone and listening to 11 options just to get an appointment within a few days.

Medicine, it appears, is still caught in the iron triangle. As William Kissick, MD, DrPH, wrote some 25 years ago in *Medicine's Dilemmas: Infinite Needs, Finite Resources,* the iron triangle of cost, quality, and access means that one cannot be increased without decreasing another. Dr. Kissick (1994) argued that to break the iron triangle, we have to disrupt the system itself, and disruption by definition is painful. The Institute for Healthcare Improvement makes a similar argument with its Triple Aim. We cannot work toward advancing one goal without advancing the others at the same time. But to date, redistributing resources to tackle inequity and reducing waste in healthcare have been beyond our political will.

There is no such thing as nondisruptive disruption. In other words, if we want to transform and democratize our healthcare delivery system, those entrenched ways of doing things will not survive. Think about the difference between how Target and Walmart handled the Amazon revolution versus how Circuit City and Sears ignored the changes in the oncoming retail revolution.

Is this an unsolvable problem? Is healthcare doomed to be the global exception to the consumer revolution? Or will it undergo disruption? Will that disruption occur because the traditional healthcare ecosystem finally gets it? Or will start-up companies and venture capitalists pull consumers into rational, friendly, and accessible platforms, with hospitals, insurers, and pharmaceutical companies being left at the station?

It's time to look ahead.

John Sculley, the former Apple CEO, tells a famous story about his early days working with Steve Jobs. Sculley told Jobs he needed a business plan to assure backers and partners. He talked about the business plan that Jobs created for Apple. This was at a time when the computer industry was stagnating. While Sculley was expecting a consultant-driven, glossy, 60-page strategic and financial plan, the entire three-year blueprint for strategic action was written on a single page—actually half a page:

- Year 1: First, we change.
- Year 2: Then, we change the industry.
- Year 3: Then, we change the world.

Steve Jobs recognized that the computer world was going through a once-in-a-lifetime change from a desktop/laptop industry to a digital lifestyle. He disrupted how the company selected, paid, and motivated employees ("we change"); he diverted dollars from the development of PowerBooks and desktop computers toward iPods and digital instruments ("we change the industry");

and, with the iPhone and iTunes store, he started the global mobile revolution ("we change the world").

Not everyone understood the strategy, either within or outside the company. Much has been written about Gateway (missing the digital computer revolution), Blockbuster (missing the streaming revolution even though it initiated it), Kodak (missing the digital camera revolution even though it invented the first portable digital camera), or traditional retail megastores underestimating the Amazon revolution.

Which brings us to healthcare. We are going through a once-in-a-lifetime disruption from a business-to-business model to a business-to-consumer model—from physician and administrator as the boss to the patient as the boss—in other words, a radically new type of health experience that works as simply and easily as most other consumer experiences. This new model is so different from the old one, we can't even call it healthcare. That label is tied to the past and is incorrect in the first place. Anyone in healthcare will tell you that we're really in a "sick care" industry designed primarily to take care of people only after they develop health problems.

We need a new term that captures the spirit of a developing concept: *health assurance*. Health assurance encompasses some of the key themes of this book:

- It gives people "health citizenship," including the right to own their medical records and the right to access care.
- It fundamentally reimagines the business of healthcare delivery to focus on health, with the services and technology aimed at ensuring we stay well, so we need as little sick care as possible.

This jump, from the past to the future, will be disruptive, and it may be painful for some. However, in an industry in which technology has advanced light-years for individual patients, healthcare delivery, the patient experience, and social determinants of health remain in the precomputer age.

YEAR 1: WE CHANGE

We are witnessing two parallel revolutions. On the one hand, people are asking for and demanding better treatment as customers of a cumbersome legacy system. On the other hand, technology, artificial intelligence (AI), and genomics will fundamentally transform how and where healthcare is provided. Real-time genomic-based decision support is already commonly used in writing drug prescriptions. Soon, many people with chronic conditions will be relying solely or in large part on virtual health assistants for wellness and management. And within ten years, a majority of all healthcare services will be delivered virtually, at home or remotely, involving AI or machine cognition applications.

To fix ourselves, we must replace the iron triangle of cost, access, and quality with a patient "diamond" of health assurance: the ability to thrive without health challenges getting in the way; the development of health-related human relationships when needed; easy navigation of one's own healthcare; and the ability to understand options that balance cost and outcomes.

At the same time, we must fix the way we select and train healthcare providers. We cannot continue to choose medical students based on their science grade point average, multiple-choice test results, and organic chemistry grades and hope that physicians will be more empathetic, communicative, and creative. Rather, choosing students based on their self-awareness, empathy, cultural competence, and communication skills is the *only* way to ensure that the "human in the middle" (the provider) is adding value to the "human at the center" (the patient) of healthcare. We need to transform the medical school experience, from the selection process to mentorship to reducing the length of study.

We also need to recognize that it will take a major cultural change for physicians to accept the Fourth Industrial Revolution (AI, 5G, the internet of things, robotics, digital twins, and so forth). It took years to get physicians and nurses to work collaboratively through interprofessional institutes and models. Soon we will need to develop "intersentient" education models between humans and nonsentient AI robots.

YEAR 2: WE CHANGE THE INDUSTRY

Our industry, although lifesaving for many, is contributing to some of society's greatest challenges. Healthcare organizations are too expensive within local, state, and federal tax and revenue structures. We contribute to inequity by perpetuating health disparities. In addition, we burden families caring for older adults, in part because providers treat end-of-life as a disease to be fixed and in part because we haven't designed simpler and less expensive ways to ensure healthy aging.

As millennials age, they will fight the system. Why millennials? Because there is little chance that, in the one-click world in which they were born and raised, millennials will accept an archaic healthcare system. There is even less chance that they will accept long waits in the waiting room, nontransparent costs and outcomes, and the inability to track and manage their own health in the same way they shop, travel, and handle every other aspect of consumer life. Before long, our current hospital-centric industry will seem as outdated as going to a bank to get money.

Here's one view of a future driven by health assurance: A company offers a subscription service to a technology-plus-human package that becomes the first layer of healthcare, a kind of pre-primary care. An individual signs up for the service and allows it to access his data, both static (e.g., DNA) and real-time (e.g., heart rate from a smartwatch, sleep patterns from an app). All of these data will be analyzed through an AI-driven predictive analytic platform that keeps track of the person's health and then observes and learns from his patterns. The technology is running in the background, constantly keeping an eye on the individual's health. If the AI spots something unusual—he isn't sleeping, his heart rate is up, or some other combination of events—it might send a text message asking some basic questions. The answers first go to an AI bot. Perhaps the person decides that not much is wrong, he's just stressed about a big decision at work. However, if the AI suspects something more, it sends the dialogue to a human physician, one who has time to talk with the person. In this way, the AI is taking over some of the low-level work that used to suck up the physician's day. She can then get on a video call with the individual and investigate his health issues.

In the very near future, providers will be paid on the basis of quality, cost, patient experience, and outcomes; hospital stays will be commoditized; physicians and nurses will coexist (and hopefully cooperate) with deep learning, machine cognition entities; we will select and educate humans (medical students) to be better humans than the robots, not better robots than the robots; and population health, predictive analytics, and social determinants will move to the mainstream of medical education and clinical care.

Moreover, technology and digital transformation will be pervasive in healthcare, and like banking, travel, and retail, most healthcare interactions will take place at or close to home. When that occurs, we truly will have "healthcare with no address."

YEAR 3: WE CHANGE THE WORLD

Changing the world is the most important part of the strategic plan, and it will require the most discussion and innovation. Spending 80 percent of our healthcare dollars on the areas that affect 20 percent of a person's health is unacceptable. Food, education, housing, prevention of chronic conditions, and combating climate change *are* healthcare! In the outdated sick-care model in which the hospital was the center of the universe, they were only part of an academic exercise. In the new health assurance model, these things become *the* most important determinants of health. Healthcare policy, healthcare incentives, and salaries will be tied to creating a healthcare system that works to prevent chronic conditions, with the patient as a partner, with technology monitoring in the background, and with most healthcare interactions happening at home.

The real test for AI engineers, technology entrepreneurs, and the healthcare ecosystem is this: Can we marshal the trillions of dollars spent in healthcare not just to develop an improved magnetic resonance imaging unit or robotic surgical arm, but also to understand how to prevent childhood obesity, eradicate smoking, prevent drug abuse and overuse of opioids, create a clean environment, and, in essence, take a no-limits approach to eradicating noncommunicable diseases? It is a future where health policy, population health, and personalized medicine converge.

CALL TO ACTION: A FRAMEWORK FOR BUILDING A CONSUMER-CENTRIC HEALTHCARE SYSTEM

Consumers want access, engagement, and value. The eight dimensions of care identified by the Picker team are as relevant today as they were 25 years ago. We know that our healthcare delivery system is not being transformed fast enough and in the right ways. Our action framework laid out in this book for healthcare leaders involves the following changes and investments (both physical and philosophical) to remove barriers, change the DNA of healthcare, and build a consumer-centric healthcare system:

- **View the CEO as chief consumer officer.** Elevate innovation as part of the mission, encourage creativity as a core value, and build the data capacity that allows design thinking to succeed. Leverage the collective knowledge and passion of the board to further the cause of building a consumer-centric culture from the top down.
- **Live the dimensions.** Know your care for every patient and identify areas in which caregiving falls short of the eight dimensions of care.

- **Look through the consumers' eyes.** Keep consumers at the center of improvement efforts. Get out from underneath measurement overload. Measure what you must to comply with value-based purchasing contracts, but spend the most time determining which metrics will get at what matters most to consumers (through direct feedback) and will help move the needle most effectively. Next, ensure that what is measured is translated into actionable and sustained improvement.

- **Be transparent.** Help consumers know what to expect along the entire journey, including treatment options, expected outcomes, and costs. Help them make decisions in the same way you would for your own family members.

- **Embrace technology.** Build competencies and capacity to gather the data you need, when you need them, and use those data, which span all eight dimensions of patient-centered care, to achieve transformational improvements in access, engagement, and value.

- **Innovate.** Determine how to meet consumers where they are. Behave like the healthcare delivery system of the future, now.

- **Gain human understanding.** Understand your patients, families, caregivers, and other consumers with greater clarity, immediacy, and depth, and ease their journey.

Let's improve healthcare, today, for everyone.

REFERENCE

Kissick, W. 1994. *Medicine's Dilemmas: Infinite Needs Versus Finite Resources.* New Haven, CT: Yale University Press.

Index

Note: Italicized page locators refer to exhibits.

Consumer-centric culture: building, 161; true, 81; at University of California, San Francisco, 112

Consumer-centric healthcare: call for, 44

Consumer-centric healthcare system, framework for, 200–201; being transparent, 201; embracing technology, 201; gaining human understanding, 201; innovation, 201; living the eight dimensions of care, 200; looking through consumers' eyes, 201; viewing CEO as chief consumer officer, 200

Consumer centricity: rationale behind premise of, xvii

Consumer-centric leadership, 151–61; anchor institutions and, 158; CEO as chief consumer officer, 153–55; changing the DNA of healthcare, 155–57; digital health technology and, 158–60; gaining human understanding and, 160–61

Consumer engagement: patient engagement vs., 40–41; provider politics and, 49

Consumer expectations: for healthcare, 54, 54–55; industries meeting or exceeding, 54, 54, 56–59

Consumer-friendly healthcare experience: creating, 26–29

Consumerism: use of term in healthcare, 107

Consumerism movement: historical factors behind rise of, 32–35

Consumer–provider relationship, building, 47–62; danger of thinking like a consumer, 62; six degrees of separation in, 47–61

Consumer revolution: grounded in human understanding, 161; need for, 193

Consumers: defining eight dimensions of patient-centered care through eyes of, 100–105, 201; healthcare attributes most sought after by, 78–79, 79; market realities and perceptions of, 48; true understanding of, 62. See also Healthcare consumers

Continuity and transition: defining through the eyes of the consumer, 103–4; as dimension of patient-centered care, 12–13, 87; at Jefferson Health, 137; at The Johns Hopkins Hospital, 119–20; in Mount Sinai Health System, 132, 136; removing barriers to, 186–87

Coordination and integration of care: at Cleveland Clinic, 122; comparison of historical and recent qualitative feedback on, 92; comparison of historical and recent quantitative feedback: dimension level, 95, 96; defining through the eyes of the consumer, 101; dimension comparison (historical and current), 95, 97, 98; as dimension of patient-centered care, 11, 87; at Jefferson Health, 137; in Mayo Clinic Health System, 115–16; in Mount Sinai Health System, 132, 135–36; removing barriers to, 180–81; at University of California, San Francisco, 109–10

Copayments, 35, 36

Cost of healthcare: consumer perceptions of, 41–42; media focus on "healthcare is broken" narrative, 50; precipitous rise in, 193

Cost sharing, 36

Cost shifting: technology advancement and, 35

COVID-19: healthcare industry transformation and, ix–x

Cow (wheeled table), 33

Crossing the Quality Chasm (Institute of Medicine), 22, 23–24

Culture: improving, through engagement and enablement, 175–77, 176

"Culture of measurement," 68

Customer-centric innovation process: adopting, 155

Cutler, David, 50

Data disorientation, 75

Data integration: employee engagement surveys and, 167

Day, George, 154, 155

Deductibles, 35, 36, 42, 52, 53, 60

Deep learning, 142

Deferment of medical treatment: cost of healthcare and, 42

"Plan of care visits": at Cleveland Clinic, 126

Population health, 158; from consumer's perspective, 100; "wellness prescriptions" and, 182–83

"Positive scoring": advantages with, 94

Premiums, 35, 52

Preventive care, 36

Preventive/screening appointment reminders: at Jefferson Health, 141

Price transparency: consumer need for, 102–3; providing tools for, 26

Princeton University: salary and employee satisfaction study, 167

Problem scoring: quality improvement efforts and, 94

Provider ratings and reviews: access to care and, 104; consumer trust and, 101–2; transparency of, 187

Quality, 76–80; consumers and value attached to, 78–79, 79; mysteriousness of, in healthcare, 43–44

Quality improvement: patients as focus of, 70

Quality measurement: foundation of, 21–24

Quality of care: consumer perceptions of, 41–42

Quick Care model (Akron Children's Hospital), 130

Quiet rooms: for staff members, 189

Raasch, Jona, 17, 18

RAND Corporation, 10

Ratings and reviews. *See* Provider ratings and reviews

Readmissions: remote monitoring and decrease in, 36

Red Box, 57

R.E.D.E. to Communicate (Cleveland Clinic), 125

Referrals: ratings and reviews and, 104

Reimbursement: outcome-based, advent of, 33; tied to patient experience, 25

Reinberger Center (Akron Children's Hospital), 131

Remote monitoring tools, 35–36

Research Triangle Institute, 10

Respect for patients' values, preferences, and expressed needs: at Akron Children's Hospital, 127, 131–32; at Cleveland Clinic, 123–24; comparison of historical and recent qualitative feedback on, 91, *92*; comparison of historical and recent quantitative feedback: dimension level, 95, *96*; defining through the eyes of the consumer, 100–101; dimension comparison (historical and current), 95, *97*, 98; as dimension of patient-centered care, 11, 87; at The Johns Hopkins Hospital, 121–22; in Mayo Clinic Health System, 113–15; qualitative research results on, 90, 91; removing barriers to, 179–80; at University of California, San Francisco, 110–12

Respite rooms, 185

Results: difficulty in sustaining, 80–81

Retail clinics, 26, 59, 104

Retail medicine: consumer revolution and, 152

Retail model: shift from wholesale model to, xvii

Retail revolution, 195

Risk-taking: encouraging, 155

Robotic medicine, 98

Robotics: physicians and, 197

Role-playing, 182

Roosevelt, Eleanor, 8

Rush Medical Center, Chicago, 113

Safety needs: in Maslow's hierarchy, *164*

Salary and employee satisfaction study, 167

Sculley, John, xx, 195

Sears, 195

Secure messaging, 34

Self-actualization: in Maslow's hierarchy, *164*, 164–65

Self-advocacy: qualitative research findings on, 90–91

Sensors, 35, 36

Shared Medical Appointments (Cleveland Clinic), 124

Shea, Greg, 154, 155

"Sick care": moving to "health assurance" from, 151

About the Authors

Ryan Donohue, corporate director of program development at NRC Health, is a thought leader in the realm of healthcare consumerism. Donohue's mission is to inspire and persuade hospital and health system leaders to embrace and engage the healthcare consumer. Over the past 15 years, he has conducted extensive research on the effects of consumerism on healthcare in the United States.

Donohue has authored several publications on healthcare consumerism, brand strategy, and effective marketing tactics. He is an adviser for The Governance Institute and a regular contributor to the *Boardroom Press* newsletter and other Governance Institute publications. He has written several articles and two white papers for The Governance Institute: *Considering the Customer: Understanding and Influencing Healthcare's Newest Change Agent,* and *Brand Equity in Healthcare: The Necessary Considerations for Brand Building in a Changing Healthcare Landscape.* He speaks regularly at Governance Institute leadership conferences and webinars, as well as at other healthcare leadership events.

NRC Health is the largest surveyor of healthcare consumers in the United States. Donohue has worked with many top health systems and hospitals to understand the changes resulting from a more consumer-centric healthcare climate. Representative clients include Mayo Clinic, Trinity Health, Baylor Scott & White Health, New York–Presbyterian Hospital, Providence, and Partners HealthCare. Donohue continues to research how consumers make decisions and how providers can move to the leading edge in consumer and patient engagement and retention.

Donohue received a BA in marketing and a BS in journalism/advertising with an emphasis in public relations from the University of Nebraska–Lincoln.

Stephen K. Klasko, MD, MBA, is an advocate for a transformation of healthcare and higher education. He has been a pioneer in using technology to build health assurance, not just sick care.

As president and CEO of Philadelphia-based Thomas Jefferson University and Jefferson Health since 2013, Dr. Klasko has led one of the nation's fastest-growing academic health institutions based on his vision of reimagining healthcare and higher education. Under his leadership, Jefferson Health expanded from 3 hospitals to 14, and the 2017 merger of Thomas Jefferson University with Philadelphia University created a preeminent professional university that includes fashion, design, architecture, and healthcare programs. He served as dean of two medical colleges and as leader of three academic health enterprises before becoming president and CEO at Jefferson.

In 2020, Dr. Klasko was named the first Distinguished Fellow of the World Economic Forum (WEF) and will co-chair the WEF Board of Stewards for The Future of the Digital Economy and New Value Creation platform. His track record of success at creating and implementing programs that are shaping the future of healthcare has earned him several other awards and recognitions: inclusion for the past three years on *Modern Healthcare*'s list of the 100 Most Influential People in Healthcare (in 2018 tied for second place); a place among *Fast Company*'s 100 Most Creative People in Business in 2018; selection as Ernst & Young's Greater Philadelphia Entrepreneur of the Year in 2018; and sixth place on *Modern Healthcare*'s list of the Most Influential Physician Executives in 2018. In 2017, his entrepreneurial leadership and success at recruiting helped Thomas Jefferson University Hospital achieve a ranking of 16th nationally—and elite honor roll status—on *U.S. News & World Report*'s Best Hospitals list.

Dr. Klasko is an obstetrician and has served as dean of two medical schools. He believes that creativity is the key skill for medical students in the age of augmented intelligence and robotics.

About the Contributors

Jona Raasch is the CEO of The Governance Institute, the leading provider of governance knowledge and solutions for CEOs and directors of hospitals and health systems.

Ms. Raasch has been involved with hospitals and health systems at all levels for the majority of her career. As the chief operating officer for NRC Health, Ms. Raasch spent 22 years helping hospitals and health systems measure and improve in the areas of quality, communication, education, and client satisfaction. She also has worked closely with a panel of industry experts whose focus is on developing and implementing initiatives to improve the patient experience.

Ms. Raasch is a member of the NRC Health advisory board and has served as an adviser to the board of the Picker Scandinavia, Germany, and Switzerland offices.

Megan Charko, MAM, is the content marketing manager at NRC Health. In this role, she leads in building a strategic plan around customer evidence. Ms. Charko works closely with clients by identifying leaders in the industry, conducting interviews, and composing case studies and articles to showcase customer success. She works closely with all teams at NRC Health to manage high-touch reference relationships across the NRC Health customer base. She leads the development and innovation spotlight production of client videos, and she researches and writes customer evidence pieces, including monthly publication of client case studies. She develops blogs, slide decks, and monthly articles featuring client testimonials.

Previously, Ms. Charko was the program manager of pediatrics at NRC Health. As such, she collaborated with pediatric organizations across the country and in Canada to coach executive leaders on best practices that support the organizational alignment of strategic initiatives with customer-focused improvement efforts. She worked with C-suite executives and directors to accelerate their improvement curve for delivering compassionate patient-centered care with greater human understanding. She harvested best practices and expanded content and resources specific to pediatric organizations. Ms. Charko also has conducted extensive research on trends of millennials as patients, as pediatric parents, and in the workplace.

In early 2017, Ms. Charko authored a nationally released white paper, *Challenging Convention: Millennial Parents' Expectations of Pediatric Care.* She also has presented at regional and national conferences and hospital associations on topics such as how healthcare organizations are changing the way they market, engage, and interact with millennials and millennial parents as consumers, as well as ways to elevate patient care with human understanding.

Ms. Charko has extensive knowledge of the Centers for Medicare & Medicaid Services Consumer Assessment of Healthcare Providers and Systems (CAHPS) programs, value-based purchasing comparative reporting, consumerism trends, and facilitating organizational relationships with various demographic groups such as patients along the entire healthcare continuum, payers, physicians, and staff.

Ms. Charko is a graduate of Nebraska Wesleyan University in Lincoln with a BS in communication studies. She earned a master of arts in management with an emphasis on leadership from Doane University in Crete, Nebraska.

Jennifer Volland, DHA, RN, FACHE, MBB, CPHQ, NEA-BC, is vice president of program development at NRC Health.

She has responsibility for harvesting best practices of healthcare organizations to drive improvement across their acute, post-acute, and Canadian programs. Additionally, Dr. Volland works closely with all of NRC Health's Magnet-designated and Magnet journey clients. Dr. Volland has worked in healthcare for more than 24 years, starting in the pediatric intensive care unit at Children's Hospital in Omaha, Nebraska. Her most recent position prior to joining NRC Health was vice president of nursing at Cancer Treatment Centers of America in Zion/Chicago. She also led the healthcare practice at Juran Institute (founded by the world renowned "Father of Quality" Dr. Joseph Juran) and created its healthcare product materials at a time when Six Sigma was shifting into healthcare. Dr. Volland has certified Six Sigma Green, Black, and Master Black Belts in the United States, England, Ireland, and Canada. She was the first individual to train and certify individuals in Six Sigma and Lean at the national level for the National Health Service in the United Kingdom.

Dr. Volland is a past president of the Nebraska and Western Iowa Chapter of the American College of Healthcare Executives (ACHE) and a past ACHE Regent for Nebraska and Western Iowa. She also has served multiple terms on the ACHE Regents Advisory Council for Nebraska and Western Iowa. In addition, she has served on the ACHE Examination Committee and Programs, Products, and Services Committee and received the ACHE Regents (Senior-Level Healthcare Executive) Award. Dr. Volland has been a Baldrige examiner, a PCORI (Patient-Centered Outcomes Research Institute) federal grant reviewer, and an American Nurses Credentialing Center content expert, and she participated on the team that reviewed and updated the NEA-BC (Nurse Executive Advanced–Board Certified) national board certification examination. Beyond working with NRC Health partners, Dr. Volland is known as an industry expert on quality and driving accelerated improvement, having conducted more than 30 best-practice topic webinars since 2012. Dr. Volland has authored or coauthored 23 peer-reviewed publications, professional organization articles, and white papers. In 2015, she received the APEX Award of Excellence in Health & Medical Writing. Her Six Sigma outcomes as a Master Black Belt have been noted in three books and a working paper. Dr. Volland has FACHE, NEA-BC, and CPHQ board certification designations, a BA in psychology from the University of Nebraska, a BS in nursing from Creighton University, an executive MBA from the University of Nebraska, and a doctor of health administration degree from Central Michigan University.

Katherine Johnson, PhD, is senior director of research and analytics at NRC Health. With almost two decades of experience in the research field, Dr. Johnson has cultivated a talent for blending scientific rigor with real-world business needs, and she strives to make research accessible and actionable for colleagues and customers. In her current role at NRC Health, Dr. Johnson leads teams of researchers and analysts across the organization while engaging in research in the area of healthcare customer loyalty. Dr. Johnson also leads NRC Health's quality and corporate compliance efforts to advance patient-centered care and ensure that the organization and its partners are operating in accordance with the protocols and guidelines set forth by the Centers for Medicare & Medicaid Services for all CAHPS surveying.

Dr. Johnson received her doctoral degree in sociology from the University of Nebraska–Lincoln, where her primary areas of focus were criminology and quantitative/qualitative methodology. She has published research briefs for NRC Health, as well as peer-reviewed journal articles and book chapters in the area of health and mental health among homeless and runaway youth.

Kathryn C. Peisert has worked in healthcare governance educational development for 16 years and is responsible for all of The Governance Institute's print and online publications, DVD/video programs, webinars, and e-learning courses. In this role, she researches and identifies key healthcare governance challenges and issues for the nation's hospital and health system boards. She researches national healthcare governance structure, culture, and best practices and also develops The Governance Institute's annual education agenda. She works with The Governance Institute's parent company, NRC Health, to develop educational publications for healthcare leaders in patient experience, cross-continuum care delivery, and consumer perceptions in the healthcare marketplace.

Previously, she served as editor with The Governance Institute and before that was a permissions and copyright editor for Roxbury Publishing Company, now a division of Oxford University Press. She has authored or coauthored articles in *Health Affairs, Journal of Health & Life Sciences Law, Prescriptions for Excellence in Health Care*, and *Healthcare Executive*, as well as numerous articles and case studies for The Governance Institute.

Ms. Peisert has a bachelor's degree in communications from the University of California, Los Angeles, and a master's degree from Boston University.